A Green Kid's Guide to
Gardening!

A Green Kid's Guide to
Watering Plants

by Richard Lay
illustrated by Laura Zarrin

magic
wagon

visit us at
www.abdopublishing.com

Looking Glass Library™ is a trademark and logo of Magic Wagon.

Printed in the United States of America, North Mankato, MN.
102012
012013
This book contains at least 10% recycled materials.

Text by Richard Lay
Illustrations by Laura Zarrin
Edited by Stephanie Hedlund and Rochelle Baltzer
Interior layout and design by Renée LaViolette
Cover design by Renée LaViolette

Library of Congress Cataloging-in-Publication Data
Lay, Richard.
  A green kid's guide to watering plants / by Richard Lay ; illustrated by Laura Zarrin.
      p. cm. -- (A green kid's guide to gardening!)
  Includes index.
  ISBN 978-1-61641-948-6
1. Gardening--Juvenile literature. 2. Plants--Water requirements--Juvenile literature. I. Zarrinnaal, Laura Nienhaus. II. Title. III. Series: Lay, Richard. Green kid's guide to gardening!
  SB457.L394 2013
  635--dc23   2012023795

Table of Contents

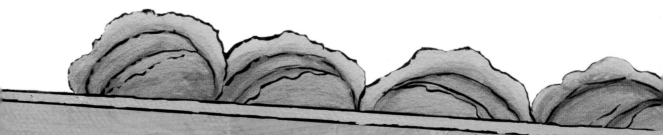

Are You Ready to Plant?

Gardeners are people who grow plants. "Being green" means learning how to live on Earth without hurting it.

You have been working hard to be a green gardener. You've built your raised bed and made compost. And, you've fertilized your soil. Now, it is time to plant and water your fruits and vegetables!

Green gardeners understand that plants need water. But, they do not waste it. Green gardeners learn how to arrange their plants to conserve water.

Study, Study, Study

A green gardener learns about plants before planting them. Different plants have different needs. Some plants need a lot of water to grow. Others need little water.

A green gardener also learns about the weather where he or she lives. Some places get a lot of rain. Others get little rain and a lot of sun. Some areas have soil that won't grow certain plants.

A green gardener grows only what is best for his or her area. Study what will grow best in your area. Then, make a list of what plants to put in your raised bed.

Where to Plant?

When you were studying, you probably noticed that plants need different amounts of water. Plants that grow on vines, such as cucumbers, need less water. Other plants, like beans, need more water.

A green gardener can conserve water by planting in groups. Grow vegetables with vines together. Grow beans in another part of the garden. Then you will not waste water on plants that may not need it.

Another way to conserve water is to grow plants in squares instead of rows. When the plants are older, their leaves touch each other. This makes a covering over the bed and reduces evaporation.

Green Gardener Tip:
Make a map of your squares so you can see where plants will grow best together. And, you'll remember what is where later!

It's Time to Plant!

To plant seeds or seedlings, first smooth the soil with a rake. Remove any rocks, sticks, or trash. Cover the soil with compost. Then water it to make it moist, but not soggy.

To plant seeds, take a small stick and make rows. Make holes the right depth for the seeds. Larger seeds should be down about one inch (3 cm). Smaller seeds should stay at the top of the soil.

It is best to put two or more seeds in each hole. That way you can be sure to get plants in every hole.

Finally, after planting the seeds or seedlings, check the soil. Do not let it dry out. Green gardeners keep soil moist.

Are They Thirsty?

Your seeds are planted and shoots are coming up. A green gardener checks the soil every day to see if the plants need water.

Plants use their roots to drink. Roots have little hairs that take water from the ground. Then the water is sent to the rest of the plant. So, plants can only get water that is underground.

Some gardeners use too much water. They waste it. This is a problem. Our planet has little water to use for people and plants.

Green gardeners understand that plants need water. But, they do not waste it. Green gardeners conserve water.

Plants Hate Showers

Some gardeners make a big mistake. They give their plants showers. They use sprinklers in the garden. But plants hate showers. They love baths.

Sprinklers put most of the water on the leaves. But, plants cannot get water through the leaves. They can only get water from the roots.

One of the best ways to get water to the roots is to use soaker hoses. These are water hoses with little holes in them. When you turn on the faucet, water slowly drips into the ground. Water then goes to the roots.

Some gardeners place their soaker hoses near where the plant goes into the ground. To use less water, green gardeners bury their soaker hoses. That way, the water comes out by the roots.

When to Give Your Plants a Drink

To check the soil, pick up a handful of dirt and squeeze it. If you can make a ball, do not add water. If you cannot make a ball, your soil is dry. It is time to water your plants.

Green gardeners water in the morning. This is when the air is cooler. So, more water gets into the ground. And, they use less water.

The amount of time you water depends on your plants and soil. After watering for a while, dig down 12 inches (30 cm) in the raised bed. If the bottom of the hole is damp, you have watered enough.

Green Gardener Tip:
Test your soil every day to keep from overwatering. If your soil sticks together, it is watered enough. Be sure to test it again the next day!

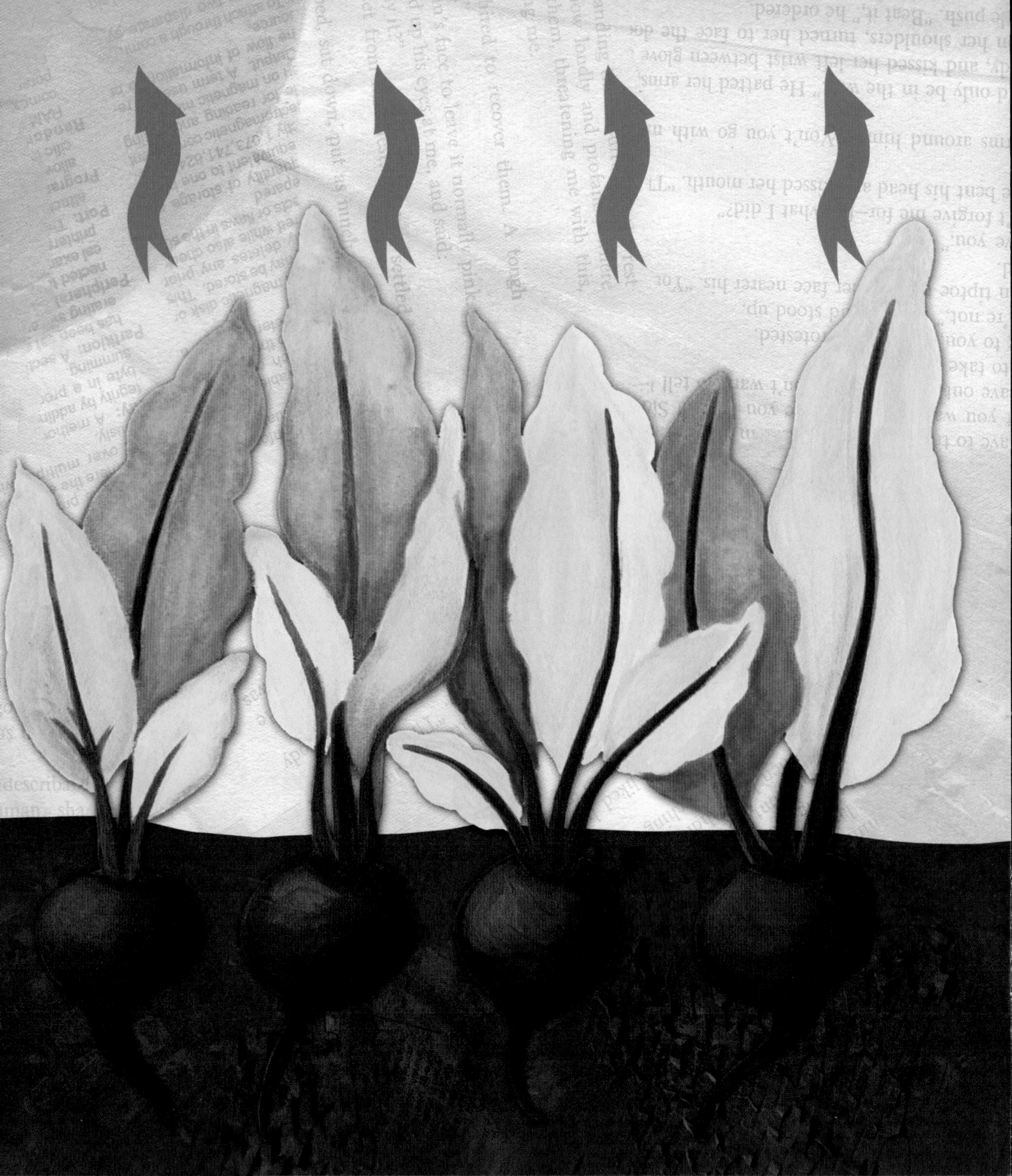

Stop Losing Water

The sun can evaporate water in the ground. It makes water hot and changes it into a gas. The gas then rises. Because of this, soil loses water.

Soil with no covering loses a lot of water. A green gardener conserves water by making a covering for the soil. You can cover the garden's soil with compost.

Another covering for your garden is mulch. Straw is good mulch. Old newspapers can be mulch. Both will help keep water in the soil.

It is important to cover soil in the fall and winter. A good covering for this time of the year is winter rye grass. It will also give plants food in the spring.

Harvest the Rain

A green gardener can also conserve water by saving rain. During the summer it may not rain very much. This is not a problem. With an adult's help you can collect rain by making a rain barrel.

A green gardener uses the water in the rain barrel to reduce the water taken from Earth. And, this water is free of chemicals that may hurt his or her plants.

You need water. Plants need water. But a green gardener does not waste water. A green gardener conserves it!

Grow Seedlings

You will need:

Clean yogurt cups	A pencil
A shallow pan	Scissors
Potting soil	Seeds
Compost	Water

Steps to grow seedlings:

1. Have an adult use scissors to make small holes in the bottom of each yogurt cup. Place the cups in a shallow pan.
2. Fill each cup with a mixture of potting soil and compost.
3. Water the soil to make it moist.
4. Use the pencil to make a hole in the soil in each cup.
5. Plant seeds in the holes. Place big seeds one inch (3 cm) deep. Place medium-sized seeds about a half inch (1 cm) deep. Place tiny seeds near the top.
6. Check the soil every day. Do not let it become dry.
7. After your seedlings appear, look for a second set of leaves. These are called the true leaves. When they appear, take the seedlings outside for a few hours every day. They need to get used to the sun, the wind, and the cooler temperatures.
8. Plant your seedlings in your garden!

Glossary

compost: decaying things that were once alive. It is used to make soil healthy.

conserve: to avoid wasteful or harmful use of something.

evaporate: to change from liquid to vapor. This process is called evaporation.

fertilizer: chemicals put into or on top of soil to make plants grow.

mulch: cut grass, straw, or other things that cover the soil in a garden.

Web Sites

To learn more about green gardening, visit ABDO Group online. Web sites about green gardening are featured on our Book Links page. These links are routinely monitored and updated to provide the most current information available.

www.abdopublishing.com

Index

SAMURAI
WARRIORS

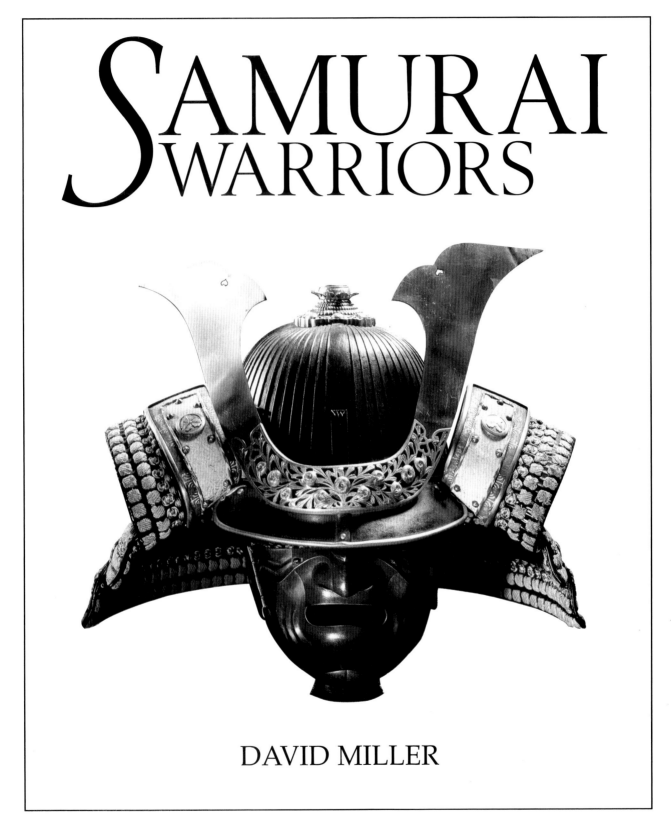

DAVID MILLER

THOMAS DUNNE BOOKS

ST. MARTIN'S PRESS ⚑ NEW YORK

A THOMAS DUNNE BOOK
An imprint of St Martin's Press

For information, address St Martin's Press, 175 Fifth Avenue, New
York, N.Y. 10010.

ISBN 0-312-24167-4

First published in the United Kingdom by Pegasus Publishing Ltd.

First US Edition

10 9 8 7 6 5 4 3 2 1

© 2000 Pegasus Publishing Ltd
High Street, Limpsfield,
Surrey RH8 0DY United Kingdom
Printed in Singapore

THE AUTHOR

David Miller is a former British Army officer, who spent his service in England, the Falkland Islands, Germany, Malaysia, the Netherlands, Scotland, and Singapore. He subsequently worked as a freelance author and worked for three years as a journalist for Jane's Information Group. Apart from numerous books on modern defence topics, he has devoted an increasing amount of time to research into historical subjects. *The Wreck of the Isabella* (Pen & Sword, 1992) was his first historical book; this book on *Samurai Warriors* is his second; and he is currently working on the life of Colonel Sir William De Lancey, who was wounded at Wellington's side at the Battle of Waterloo in June 1815. His interest in Japanese history was aroused by a *samurai* sword brought back by his father from his service in the Far East in 1944-45, and this book is the result.

Editor: Ray Bonds
Designer: Megra Mitchell
Photo research: Tony Moore
Colour reproduction: Acumen Overseas PTE Ltd
Printed and bound in Singapore

CONTENTS

Introduction

"**S**amurai" is one of those words which is known around the world and which needs no translation into other languages. It denotes a specifically Japanese warrior, who followed a very particular code — *bushido*. Much about these men is shrouded in mystery and legend, and the story has been affected by the reappearance of the *samurai* ethos and of the (so-called) *hara-kiri* suicide pilots in the Second World War. But, exactly who were these men? What did they stand for, and what did they achieve? Were all these stories about ritual suicide really true? This book sets out to provide some of the answers to those questions, and seeks, also, to place the *samurai* in the correct context. To begin with, however, it is important to clarify two matters which sometimes cause confusion: the names of Japanese people, and the separate issues of massacres and ritual suicide.

JAPANESE NAMES

Japanese names follow conventions which are quite different from those followed in the West and they often cause confusion. At the very top, the emperor had no family name, needing none because the dynasty never changed. Indeed, until 1872 it was forbidden for his subjects either to pronounce or to write the name of the living emperor and he was simply referred to in speech as "the present emperor", while in writing the name a stroke had to be omitted from each character.

Starting in 415 AD Japanese nobles followed the Chinese style and carried a family name, which comes first, followed by the individual's given name. Thus, Obata Toramori, for example, was Toramori of the Obata family, and his son was Obata Masamori. Also in earlier times, the names of nobles were sometimes written Minamoto-no-Yoritomo (= Yoritomo of the Minamoto family), where "no" is simply the genitive participle (ie, "of").

Peasants were not permitted to have family names until 1872, although in earlier times an *ashigaru* (foot soldier) could earn *samurai* rank, one privilege of which was to be allowed to take a family name.

A very few historical individuals were so important that they are remembered only by their given names, there being no possibility of confusing them with anyone else. Thus, Tokugawa Ieyasu is remembered, simply, as 'Ieyasu,' Toyotomi Hideyoshi as "Hideyoshi" and Minamoto Yoritomo as "Yoritomo".

A further complication was the custom of changing names at different stages of life. Hideyoshi, for example, was the son of a peasant named Yasuke and was given the name Hiyoshi-maro by his mother. When he enlisted as a soldier he did so under the name of Kinoshita Tokichiro, but when he became a general he, at a whim, took the name of Hashiba. Then, when he was appointed Kuambaku, the emperor granted him a patent of a family name, "Toyotomi", which was passed down to his descendants.

ABOVE: Three authentic samurai (photographed in the 1870s) show examples of their traditional dress, weapons and armour. All carry the two swords, which were the emblems of their status.

DEATHS

The stories told in this book are littered with examples of massacres, particularly after a battle, where the victorious army quite deliberately annihilated every member of the opposing force or clan that could be found. Similarly, at the end of sieges, especially if they had been protracted and involved heavy fighting, the conquerors often sacked the castle or city, once again killing every last man, woman and child they could set their hands on. These were bloody and brutal events by modern standards, but they must be seen in the context of their times and they certainly bear comparison with similar events in European warfare.

For example, in 1571 the Japanese *samurai* general, Oda Nobunaga, set out to break the power of the warrior monks in their monastery complex at Hiei. After a very brief siege, Nobunaga's men set out to kill every single person inside the fortress — some 20,000 men, women and children in all. But this should be compared with the behaviour of Hernando Cortez, the Spanish conquistador, who sacked the Aztec city of Tenochtitlan in 1521, just 50 years earlier. Cortez's men were directly responsible for the death, by killing, starvation or disease, of some 100,000 inhabitants of that city. Similarly, beheading was a common practice in Japan, but it is worth remembering that it continued until the 17th Century in England and until the early 19th Century in France.

One facet of *samurai* culture which causes surprise in Europe and America is the concept of ritual suicide (*seppuku*), a practice that appears alien to Western eyes. The idea of a man (and sometimes a woman) calmly pulling a dagger through his stomach before stretching his neck to allow a comrade to behead him is certainly difficult to comprehend. On the other hand, an "honourable suicide" is by no means unknown in most European cultures even in the 19th and 20th Centuries, especially in the armed forces. where it was made clear to an officer that he had committed an offence — either military or social — for which the only solution was to take the "honourable course" and shoot himself. This usually took the form of directing the officer to a room where a revolver, containing a single round, was lying on a table. Indeed, as recently as 1944, in one of the most disgraceful of such episodes, a German general handed Field Marshal Rommel, who was implicated in the Bomb Plot against Hitler, a phial of poison with instructions that he was to take it.

BELOW: A scene from the depiction of the true story, known as the "Forty-seven Ronin", and is immortalised in the story Chishungura (=treasury of loyal hearts). Here the conspirators, intent on avenging their dead master, break into the house of their victim, Kira, at dead of night.

In European navies, also, a tradition developed in the 19th Century that a captain's responsibility for his ship was so complete that if the ship was lost, either in action or through culpable accident, then the captain was "expected to go down with his ship". This was practised by various British and German captains — and, in some cases, by admirals, as well — in both World Wars and excited a degree of popular understanding; it certainly did not earn an official condemnation. Whatever the justification (or lack of it) for these European practices, the end result was the same as for the Japanese — the man had taken his own life.

Chapter 1

THE SETTING
GEOGRAPHY AND CLIMATE

BELOW: Japan's four main islands, lying off the east coast of Asia, are of extremely rugged and mountainous terrain.

The Japanese archipelago comprises four main islands — Hokkaido, Honshu, Kyushu and Shikoku — and over 3,000 smaller ones, stretching in a great crescent some 2,400 miles (3,800km) long from Sakhalin Island in the north to the southern tip of Korea in the south. These islands, some 150,000 square miles (390,000sq km) in area, are the visible tip of a great mountain range that rises from the Pacific floor and includes 186 volcanoes, of which about a third are "active," erupting from time

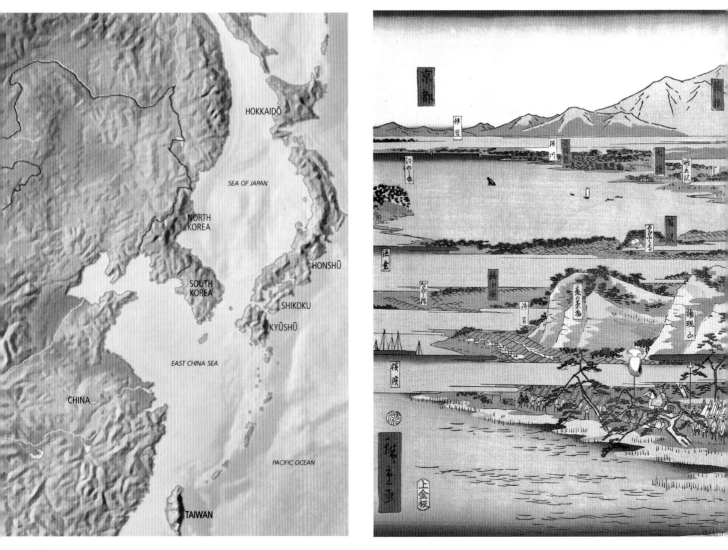

to time. Earthquakes are far more frequent, with approximately 1,500 earth tremors per year, of which the great majority are very minor and barely perceptible, but there is a severe earthquake, almost inevitably involving heavy loss of life, about once every two-three years. Japanese folklore abounds with stories of devastating earthquakes in which villages and towns have been either shaken or engulfed, and they have been an inescapable feature of everyday life throughout Japanese history.

The main islands are noted for their rugged terrain and some 75 percent of the land can be described as mountainous, with Honshu, the largest island, being about the same size as Great Britain. Throughout its history Japan has had only two major resources in abundance — timber and water — and only about 20 percent of the land has ever been fit for farming. As a result, the internal wars which are such a central feature of Japanese history have, whatever the overt reason, usually been about "land." That land was owned by groups of related families (clans), each headed by a chief, and it was the struggle for control of that land that eventually gave rise to the warriors known as *samurai*.

In the highlands, the majority of rivers are short, fast flowing, tend to cause floods, and are of little value for navigation. In the plains, however, there are a few larger rivers, which yield an abundance of fish and are navigable, although this inevitably means that they provide major obstacles to military operations.

Most of the Japanese archipelago has a moderate climate, Hokkaido with cool summers and cold winters and Honshu warm, humid summers, with mild winters in the south and sharper in the north. The two smaller islands have long hot summers and mild winters. All of Japan has a high rainfall, with two seasons of heavy rain, following the pattern of the Asian monsoon. In the western mountains winter snow collects to such a depth that spring floods are extremely difficult to control. Even without the complications of war, the Japanese people

A daimyo, *accompanied by the usual large retinue, proceeds along the* Tokaido. *Everything relating to such progresses was carefully regulated by the* shogunate.

have always had to contend with these geographical and climatic problems and natural disasters such as floods, typhoons, and tidal waves have claimed large numbers of casualties every year since time immemorial.

COMMUNICATIONS

During the *samurai* period travel was by foot, carriage or palanquin and there were two principal roads, which were of great strategic importance both connecting the two great cities of Kyoto and Edo. These highways started at the *Sanjo* bridge in Kyoto and passed along the southern shore of Lake Biwa, but then they split. The first of these great highways, the *Nakasendo* (= central mountain road), ran through the mountains, a distance of some 380 miles (611km), during which it traversed nine passes, the highest of which was 5,590 feet (1,700m) above sea level; it is believed to have been in use since the 8th Century AD. The other road, the *Tokaido*, followed the coastline, through Hamamatsu and Shizuoka. Both were repeatedly fought over, ownership being exercised through control of a series of castles and guarded barriers.

Ieyasu (1542-1616), the first Tokugawa *shogun*, devoted huge energies to improving the road system. Thus, as a result of his programmes, the most important route, the *Tokaido*, had 53 *shiki* (= way-stations), each of which had hotels, pack-horses, baggage-coolies, and palanquin bearers. The procedures to be observed and the prices to be charged were laid down in minute detail. Mountain roads such the *Nakasendo* were also improved, as were bridges and ferries, and all roads were marked with small hillocks at every *ri* (approximately 2.4 miles [3.9km]). Main roads had to be 36 feet (11m) wide and lined with poplars, minor roads 18 feet (5.5m) wide, and tracks 3 feet (1m) wide.

Such was the military importance of the major routes that *seki* (= guarded gates) were erected at inter-province boundaries and on the major mountain passes. They were also erected at the frontier between Japanese-held territory and that held by the Ainu, to maintain the distinction between the two. All such gates were under constant military guard and travellers required a passport or password to pass through them. Many Japanese novels, dramas, and legends centre upon the ruses employed to fool the guards into allowing travellers to talk their way past the guards on a *seki*.

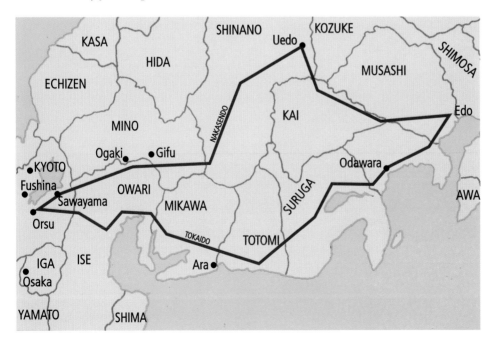

LEFT: The two main highways, Nakasendo *and* Tokaido, *connecting the two great cities of Kyoto and Edo, were both frequently fought over, and a series of castles and guarded barriers were built to aid control of them.*

THE HISTORY OF JAPAN

The Japanese people have always had a very keen sense of their history, which goes back longer than that of most countries, although the further back in time, the less reliable the information about it is. However, it is important to see the *samurai* within their national historical context, which in general terms, can be divided into three major periods:

LEGENDARY – From the remotest times to about 60 AD.

PRE-HISTORY— From about 60 AD to 500 AD.
HISTORIC — From 500 AD onwards.

THE JŌMON PERIOD: CA 10,000-300 BC

The original habitation of the Japanese islands has been traced as far back as 4,500 BC, when they were sparsely inhabited by farmers, hunters, and fishermen of a culture known as *Jōmon* (= cord pattern), so-called because the pottery they produced was decorated with rope-like designs. Researches also indicate that a Caucasian race called the Ainu were the first true inhabitants. They appear to have entered the island of Hokkaido from the Sakhalin peninsula, where their descendants exist to this day.

According to Japanese cultural tradition, the country's history began in precisely 660 BC, when the first emperor, Jimmu Tenno (1), came to the throne.[1] According to the chronicle *Nihon shoki*, written in 720 AD, Jimmu was of divine descent and established his rule on Kyushu before leading his troops northward into the central Honshu province of Yamato. Once they had settled there, the name Yamato was selected as the family name of the Imperial house and eventually came to be applied to all of ancient Japan.

Again according to legend, Emperor Keiko (12) was physically tall and strong, and became the first person to bear the title *shogun* (= barbarian-subduing general). The legends continue, however, that Keiko's favorite son, Yamato Daké, was not only cunning, fearless, and proficient in the martial arts, but also that he was even stronger than his father, to the extent that he actually tore his brother apart in a quarrel. Yamato Daké took part in several expeditions against the Ainu, but then died young and many believe that he was the role model for the later *samurai*. By the early centuries AD the Yamato exercised control over a large number of tribes, each with its own territory and its own gods, but the Yamato's principal deity, *Amaterasu-o-mikami* (= heaven-illuminating [ie, sun] goddess), was worshipped by all.

THE YAYOI PERIOD: 300 BC TO 250 AD

During the Yayoi period, which lasted from about 300 BC to 250 BC, a new group became predominant; what they called themselves is not known, but their modern name is the "Yayoi", after the village where their pottery was first discovered. The Chinese chronicle, *Wei Chih*, which was written about 300 AD, refers to trading during the Yayoi period with Wa (Japan), where one of the tribal federations was Yamataikoku (Yamato), ruled by a warrior-queen named Himiko. According to the Chinese, her magical capabilities had enabled her to attain power in about 190 AD, following which she retired to a strongly held fortress to be tended by a retinue of 999 women and one man, conducting affairs of state through her brother. This was the first known example of the type of "cloistered government" which was to recur in later Japanese history. Himiko died at some time in the middle of the 3rd Century but, despite the evidence, she is not included in the official list of Japanese emperors and empresses regnant.

THE KOFUN PERIOD: 250 - 600 AD

This period is named after the large and distinctive burial mounds (*kofun*), which were originally used only for members of the ruling class, but later also for commoners. This appears to have been a sophisticated and militaristic society, based on an army in which the troops wore armour and carried swords and — following the introduction of horses to Japan in the second half of the 4th Century — rode horses, as well.

This period represents a critical stage in Japan's evolution towards a more cohesive and recognized state, the most developed region being in Kinai (roughly, an area centred on modern Osaka) and the easternmost part of the Inland Sea (*Seto Naikai*). The period also saw

ABOVE: Jimmu, first in the "official" list of emperors, reigned from 660-585 BC and is shown in full war regalia, seated on the chair from which he commanded his troops.

[1] The names of Japanese emperors and the dates of their rule appear on an "official" list published by the Imperial Household Agency. In this book the names of all emperors and empresses regnant are followed by their number on that list and their dates can be ascertained by reference to the Appendices.

御誂屋敷幟内
袖宮后皇
武内大臣

ABOVE: Empress Jingu who not only ordered but also led the first invasion of Korea, with her minister, Takeuchi.

power concentrated in a few, large clans, each of which was headed by a patriarch, one of whose responsibilities was to perform the sacred rites to the clan's *kami* (sacred spirit), thus ensuring, it was hoped, the clan's long-term welfare.

Emperor Chuai's (14) successor, his widow, Empress Jingu (15), ordered the invasion of Korea, a very ambitious undertaking for those times. It was, in effect, a short-term naval raid, but it had an unexpected and unintended outcome, since it exposed the Japanese court to Korean culture (which was itself heavily influenced by neighbouring China). One innovation made by Jingu herself, and based on what she had learnt in Korea, was to recast the divisions of her empire into five "home provinces" (*Go kinai*) and seven regions (*do*), a geographical arrangement which has survived, with only the most minor amendments, down to modern times. Over the following centuries intercourse between Korea and Japan, which included the movement of people, spurred intellectual development in Yamato, so much so that Chinese literature and philosophy became popular at the court of Yamato, resulting in Chinese script being taken into use at the beginning of the 5th Century.

Another event of major significance came in 552 AD, with the arrival of Buddhist priests from Korea, who not only brought religious teachings, but also calendars and methods of keeping time. Although the Japanese were expelled from Korea in 562 AD, this imported culture quickly established strong roots and, in a similar manner to the spread of Christianity in Europe, Buddhism gradually extended its hold, particularly after it was embraced by Emperor Yomei (31). It then became a powerful philosophy for the whole elite, including rulers and warriors, resulting in the abandonment of the *kofun*, first by the aristocracy in about 600 AD, although their use by commoners, especially in the outlying areas, continued to about 800 AD.

THE ASUKA PERIOD: 550-710
The next phase in the development of the Yamato state was the Asuka period, so called because various imperial capitals were established in the Asuka region, the first in about 590 AD. Such moves were necessary because of the prevailing belief that a death so polluted the house in which it took place that it had to be abandoned and, since the emperor was so much more important, it followed that his death polluted the entire capital city. This meant that one of each new emperor's earliest tasks was to establish a new capital, presumably at no small inconvenience to those involved. The period also saw a further flowering of the arts, together with social and political progress, continuing the trends of the Kofun period.

Politically, the Yamato court exercised increasing authority over the clans on Kyushu and Honshu, acquiring land and conferring titles on vassals, until the Yamato name became synonymous with the state itself. These territories were ruled through a network of counties by state-appointed administrators, while the lower classes were organized into functional groups, such as armourers, artisans, farmers (the most numerous), fishers, potters, weavers, and so on.

At the court there came the first example of a pattern which was to recur throughout Japanese history, in which one clan, in this case the Soga, achieved a position of predominance, enabling its leading members to marry into the Imperial family, and, ultimately, to start

LEFT: *Prince Shotoku (574-622 AD) was a great reformer. On the left is a script in his own hand; on the right a picture of "Prince Shotoku With Two Pages" painted circa 800 AD.*

dictating state policy. Thus, in 587 AD, the head of the clan, Soga-no-Umako, was able to install his nephew, Sushun (32), as emperor. Sushun, however, then showed a degree of independence by, first, opposing the spread of Buddhism, and then by starting to plan to curb Umako's power. On discovering this, Umako had his nephew assassinated and replaced by Empress Suiko (33), although real power was exercised by others, principally Shotoku Taishi (574-622 AD), who was Prince Regent from 593 to 622 AD.

Shotoku, one of the great reformers in Japanese history, was deeply influenced by Confucian principles, including the concept of the Mandate of Heaven, which postulated that the emperor or empress regnant ruled under the authority of a supreme force. Shotoku introduced systems of rank and new forms of etiquette, while his *Kenpo jushichiju* (= seventeen-article constitution), enacted in 604 AD, sought to bring harmony into a society which, in Confucian terms, was almost totally lacking in structure. Shotoku was a devoted student of Chinese culture and not only established formal diplomatic relations between the two countries, but also despatched students to China to learn about Buddhism and Confucianism. He was also responsible for the building of numerous Buddhist temples, as well as major public works, including a system of national highways.

A series of court intrigues came to a head in 645 AD with a revolt against the Soga clan's rule, led by Prince Naka and Nakatomi-no-Kamatari, who had the head of the clan, Soga-no-Iruka, murdered at a banquet. The rebels introduced the *Taika* Reform (*taika* = great change),

LEFT: *The Horyuji, said to have been built by Shotoku Taishi for his father, the Emperor Yomei, still survives more or less intact at Ikaurga, 10 miles south west of the present Nara City.*

ABOVE: Fujiwara-no-
Michinaga (966-1027), who
married five of his daughters to
emperors and had three
emperors as grandsons, as
depicted in the Murasaki
Shikiby Diary.

establishing the *ritsuryo* systems (= codes or maxims of behaviour) which endured for some three centuries. Again, Chinese influences predominated and the rulers made the people direct subjects of the throne: clan chiefs' titles and land tenure ceased to be hereditary, reverting to the state on the tenant's death. New taxes were introduced and, to enable the country to be administered more effectively, it was divided into provinces, each with a centrally appointed governor, with each province being sub-divided in its turn into districts and villages.

The *ritsuryo* system was refined in the *Taiho Ritsuryo* (= Great Treasure Code) of 701 AD which further strengthened the Chinese-style central administration through a Department of Rites, which was responsible for *Shinto* and court rituals, and a Department of State, which consisted of eight ministries: central administration, ceremonies, civil affairs, imperial household, justice, military affairs, people's affairs, and the treasury. A Chinese-style civil service examination system based on the Confucian classics was also adopted, although aristocratic birth continued to be the main qualification for higher positions.

THE NARA PERIOD: 710-794

Implementing the *Taiho Ritsuryo* required a large central bureaucracy and it was eventually accepted that the system of moving following the death of the emperor was no longer practicable. As a result, a permanent capital was established at Nara (Heijokyo), some 20 miles east of Osaka, in 710 AD, where the number of inhabitants rapidly grew to some 200,000, approximately 10,000 of whom were government bureaucrats. This central government did, however, set a number of nationwide improvements in train, such as more improvements to the road system and the issue of a coinage, although these had to be accompanied by a more efficient tax-collecting system. But, as was inevitable in an era of poor communications, the further from the capital the less effective these reforms proved to be and regional lords began to amass large estates (known as *shoen*), forcing many agricultural workers to leave the land. Centralized control became increasingly weak and, in an effort to reassert it, the capital was moved, but this time for administrative rather than spiritual reasons, first to Nagaoka (in 784) and then again in 794, when Emperor Kammu (50) moved it to the city of Heian-kyo, which offered a number of advantages, including good sea and land access.

THE HEIEAN PERIOD: (795-1198)

When the 9-year old Emperor Seiwa (56) acceded to the throne in 858, his maternal grandfather, Fujiwara Yoshifusa, became regent, enabling the Fujiwara clan to assume control of most of the court and administrative offices. They also forced the Imperial family to adopt a more secluded lifestyle, leaving real power to be exercised by the Fujiwara family, whose pre-eminence lasted for three centuries. Fujiwara Mototsune became the first official civil dictator (*kampaku*) in 884 AD, but the greatest of the clan was Michinaga, whose five daughters married successive emperors. This Fujiwara period saw a great flowering of Japanese culture, which continued to be influenced, although by no means dominated, by China. The dictatorship of Michinaga (995-1027) is regarded as the classical age of Japanese literature. By about 1070 Heian's name had been changed to Kyoto (= capital city), a name it has retained to this day, despite its subsequent loss of status when the capital moved to Yedo (Tokyo).

Signs of impending collapse increased. The 10th Century saw rebellions in the eastern provinces by Taira Masakado, while a pirate, Fujiwara Sumitomo, established himself in the Inland Sea. These were both put down in the early 940s, but a long-running frontier war against the Emishi people in the north of Honshu rumbled on. These were followed by the Early Nine Years War (1051-1062) in which the Abe clan, led by Abe Sadato, was brought back under Imperial control by government forces led by Minamoto Yoriyoshi, aided by his son, Minamoto Yoshiie. The main engagement was the Battle of Kawasaki (1057), where the Minamoto attacked a strong position in a blizzard and were repulsed, but they then conducted a fighting withdrawal in which Yoshiie greatly distinguished himself. Yoshiie was the commander in the Later Three Years War (1086-1088) which resulted in the defeat of the forces of the Kiyowara clan, led by Kiyowara Iehira. These two campaigns are of particular significance, in that they mark the first appearance of the group of professional warriors, which came to be known as the *samurai*.

ABOVE: A section from a scroll depicting the Go-sannen Gassen *(Later Three Years' War), which lasted from 1086 to 1088, and resulted in the defeat of the Kiyowara clan.*

Emperor Daigo (60) exercised direct rule in an effort to thwart the Fujiwara clan, but following his death in 930 AD the Fujiwara exerted increasing control over the court and by the year 1000 Fujiwara Michinaga was a virtual dictator. Despite this, there was a flowering of cultural and artistic activity, with particular emphasis on Japanese, as opposed to Chinese, forms.

The Imperial court existed in an atmosphere where the principal aim was to achieve a pinnacle of aesthetic perfection. The courtiers' world was dominated by beauty, poetry, and art, with the role of the people being simply to provide the money which made it all possible. The *samurai* did whatever fighting was required, settling the aristocrats' quarrels on their behalf.

As inevitably happens, two trends became discernible: the longer Fujiwara rule continued the more corrupt it became; and the further from the capital the weaker the control exercised

*LEFT: The interior of the Sanjusangendo temple, erected by Taira-no-Kiyormori (1118-1181), which houses one thousand statues of the Bodhisattva Avalokitesvara (*Kannon *in Japanese).*

by central government. As a result, the hereditary fiefdoms, originally granted as payment for official positions, became increasingly powerful, with the Taira in the southwest and the Minamoto in the east forming local groups of warriors for mutual protection. By the 12th Century the power of these two military clans extended to the court itself, where a struggle for control of the empire ensued.

In 1155 the Emperor Konoe (76) died at the age of 17 years, an unexpected event which had calamitous consequences, since the succession had not been clarified. The naming of Go-Shirikawa (77) caused serious disturbances, giving rise the following year to what became known as the *Hogen-no-Ran* (Hogen Incident) in which two rival groups of *samurai* fought each other in the streets of Kyoto over the course of one disastrous and bloody night. The Shirakawa-den palace was attacked by *samurai* led by Minamoto-no-Yoshitomo, who overcame their rivals led by Minamoto Tametomo. The engagement consisted mostly of arrow duels, but ended with the palace being set alight and destroyed.

This was followed in 1160 by the *Heiji-no-Ran* (Heiji Incident), in which Minamoto-no-Yoshitomo took advantage of the temporary absence of Taira-no-Kiyomori from the capital to storm the Senjo palace. Yoshitomo's *samurai* captured both Emperor Nijo (78) and his father, the "cloistered emperor," Go-Shirakawa (77), and murdered Michinori. On learning of these events, Kiyomori hastened back to the capital, but in the meantime the emperor and his father, the former disguised as a maidservant, had escaped. Yoshitomo and his men were then quickly overcome.

The Taira leader, Kiyomori, was named prime minister in 1167 and for a time Taira rule appeared secure, but in 1180 Minamoto Yoritomo started a new civil war — the Gempei War — in eastern Japan. The Minamoto defeated the Taira at the Battle of Yashima (1184) but most of the Taira escaped. The war culminated in the Battle of Dan-no-Ura (1185), a naval battle in which the Taira were decisively defeated. Losses during the fighting were severe, but then most of those who survived committing suicide. This established Yoritomo as the leader of Japan, ending the era of imperial administration and inaugurating a military dictatorship that ruled the nation for the next seven centuries. Yoritomo, however, had some unfinished business, since his brother Yoshitsune, uncle Yoshiie, and cousin Yoshinaka, were proving too successful and he had them all murdered, a crime which he immediately blamed on the remaining Fuijiwara, thus giving himself the excuse he needed to destroy them utterly.

THE FIRST SHOGUNATE: *KAMAKURA BAKUFU (1185-1333)*

In 1192 the emperor appointed Yoritomo *sei-i taishogun* (= barbarian-subduing great general [usually shortened to *shogun*]), a title which had been conferred before, but the significant difference this time was that it was with hereditary rights. Confirmed in his power, Yoritomo established his capital at Kamakura, which became the seat of actual power – known, not always, courteously, as *bakufu* – leaving the emperor and his court at Kyoto. As the effective commander-in-chief, Yoritomo installed a military governor (*shiugo*) in each of five provinces, and, when this had been accepted, he placed one in all the other provinces – all, of course, his relatives and beholden to him. He also extended the imperial domain, but with the emperor himself firmly relegated to the role of figurehead, while the imperial courtiers, despite their imposing titles, remained powerless. The feudal system was developed and it was a period of increased social status and economic power for the *samurai*, who began the practice of meditation to induce a proper state of mind.

New institutions were now needed in the face of social, economic, and political changes as the *Taiho* Code lapsed, its institutions relegated to ceremonial functions, while the most powerful family, the Fujiwara, governed Japan and determined the general affairs of state, such as succession to the throne. Land ownership became the main preoccupation of the aristocracy, not so much because direct control by the imperial family or central government had declined, but more from strong family solidarity and a lack of a sense of Japan as a single nation.

At the start of the 13th Century a new family, the Hojo, rose to power. They claimed descent from Emperor Kammu (50) and had taken the name of their main settlement, Hojo, as their family name. The Hojo had supported and eventually intermarried with the Minamoto, but they then became even more ambitious. The seventh in this line, Hojo Tokimasa, employed a series of murders and conspiracies to eliminate the Minamoto heirs and their supporters, thus making the Hojo the military rulers of Japan, although no member of the family ever became *shogun*. Instead, the family prevailed upon the emperor to appoint a figurehead *shogun*, leaving a Hojo to govern as *shikken*, or regent. Between 1199 and 1333 there were 12 Hojo *shikkens*

(Tokimasa, Yoshitoki, Yasutoki, Tsunetoki, Tokiyori, Masatoki, Tokinune, Sadatoki, Morotoki, Hirotoki, Takatoki and Moritoki), who, in a curious arrangement, wielded the real power on behalf of the *shogun*, who was, supposedly, ruling in the name of the emperor. The Hojos made and broke *shoguns*, as, in other times, *shoguns* appointed and deposed emperors.

In 1274 and again in 1281 the Mongols, who by then controlled both China and Korea, carried out two invasions of Japan. These invasions were unsuccessful but turned out to be a serious drain on Hojo resources, as the rulers found themselves unable to reward their vassals for the support they had given. Sensing his rival's weakness, Go-Daigo (96), an able emperor, led a rebellion that climaxed in 1333 with the capture of Kamakura, leading to the total downfall of the Hojo.

Some Hojo rulers proved to be enlightened, encouraging art and literature and leading the resistance to the Mongol invasions, but others proved cruel and vicious rulers and their departure was unlamented. Indeed, a particularly unpleasant insect was named the "Hojo bug" and for many centuries one day a year was set aside for a mass hunt and killing of these pests.

THE SECOND SHOGUNATE: *ASHIKAGA BAKUFU (1336-1574)*

Go-Daigo proved less successful in his efforts to restore the imperial administration and in 1336 was driven out of his capital, Kyoto, by one of his former vassals, Ashikaga Takauchi (1305-1358). Takauchi installed his own candidate for emperor, Kogon (North 1), while Go-Daigo and his supporters fled to Yoshino, in Honshu, but taking the imperial regalia with them, thus starting the great imperial schism. Japan was ravaged by a bitter civil war for 56 years as Go-Daigo and his successors fought the Ashikaga *shoguns* and their puppet emperors. Finally, in 1392, an Ashikaga envoy persuaded the true emperor at Yoshino, Go-Kameyama (99), to abdicate and relinquish the sacred imperial regalia, thus enabling the Ashikaga *shoguns* to claim their emperor as the rightful ruler and to establish their own control over all Japan. By this time, however, the *daimyos* had established themselves in all parts of the country and the Ashikaga *shoguns* never managed to impose their control over these hereditary, feudal lords, who attacked their neighbours and seized land.

In general, this period of Ashikaga ascendancy saw the further development of Buddhism as a political force, accompanied by major achievements in art and literature. Indeed, culture flourished, with the development of *ikebana*, *bonsai* and, in particular, the tea ceremony, which was governed by tradition and seen as both a spiritual expression and a mental exercise. Other major cultural achievements included the *Noh* play, landscape painting, architecture, scroll painting, and poetry.

There was also, however, a rise in the wealth and power of the Buddhist monasteries, which became major forces in the country. Monks, often clad in armour and bearing weapons, were able to turn the tide of battles with their strong organizations and fortified monasteries. By the 16th Century local wars among feudal lords had become endemic and the period is still remembered in Japanese history as the "Epoch of a Warring Country". It started with the Onin War in 1467 and continued until 1568, by which time the authority and prestige of both the emperor and the *shogun* had decreased markedly.

THE THIRD SHOGUNATE: TOKUGAWA DYNASTY (1603-1867)

Three great warlords eventually re-established order. Oda Nobunaga (1534-1582), a general of the Taira clan, broke the power of the monasteries over the years 1570 to 1580, ending Buddhism as a political force. Then Toyotomi Hideyoshi (1536-1598), a follower of Oda, united all Japan under his rule by 1590 and marked out the boundaries of all feudal fiefs. Hideyoshi was also responsible for two invasions of Korea, the first in 1592, the second in 1597. The motives for these two massive expeditions – the first Japanese military adventures abroad since Empress Jingu's invasion of Korea in 200 AD – remain unclear. They may have been a deliberate attempt to expand overseas trade, but it seems more likely that Hideyoshi had simply run out of enemies in Japan and was looking for new conquests. Because of his humble beginnings, Hideyoshi could not be appointed *shogun* so a new title, *kuambaku* (= regent of the emperor), was conferred on him in 1586, instead.

When Tokugawa Ieyasu attained power, however, he understood that, although the post of *kuambaku* was second only to the emperor, it had no direct authority to direct the army. He had to become *shogun*, which he achieved in 1603. He established his military government at Edo (modern-day Tokyo), where he built a great castle, which was soon surrounded by a thriving metropolis of more than a million inhabitants. Having established the *shogunate*, he abdicated, transferring the office of *shogun* to his son, Tokugawa Hideie, although Ieyasu

BELOW: Oda Nobunaga (1534-1582) installed Ashikaga Yoshiaki as shogun in 1568, but later deposed him again, assuming the post himself. He was responsible for the annihilation of the monks at Mount Hiei, effectively ending the power of the monasteries.

RIGHT: A samurai *strolls along a street, followed by his servant carrying his paraphernalia and umbrellas. On the right a peasant prostrates himself in homage, but the* samurai *turns his head away in disdain.*

ABOVE: Tokugawa Ieyasu (1542-1616) was appointed shogun *in 1603, setting up his* bakufu *(military government) in Edo, from where his descendants ruled Japan until the Meiji Restoration in 1868.*

continued to be active in state affairs, and personally led the army which attacked Osaka Castle in 1615.

Ieyasu carried through many reforms, completing the feudal reorganization begun by Hideyoshi, with all *daimyos* and administrators, as well as the emperor and his court, under the firm control of the *shogunate*. His strictures were such that *daimyos* needed permission to do almost anything of importance, including taking on additional vassals, repairing their castles, entering the land of other lords, or arranging daughters' marriages. He also ordained that all *daimyos* had to build a residence at Edo, to live there for a large part of every year and that their wives and children were to remain in Edo during the *daimyos*' absence.

Society as a whole was divided into four classes — *samurai*, peasants, artisans, merchants — and there was virtually no movement between these strata, with the national code emphasizing the duty of all to respect and honour those above them on the social ladder. The military element was pre-eminent and only *samurai* were allowed to wear two swords: the short one at all times, but the long one only outdoors. Above them all was the emperor, who was treated with honour, but the real power lay in the hands of the *shogun*. Thus, during this period, the social structure became rigidly stratified and Japan became isolated from the outside world.

The relatively peaceful Tokugawa ascendancy presented a real problem to the *samurai*, who found themselves without a battle to fight and thus without a *raison d'etre*. Some were forced to give up their status as *samurai* and to "lower" themselves to undertake professions such as farming or trading, while others became *ronin* (ie, *samurai* without masters).

The government tried to help unemployed *samurai* by stressing the importance of education, and Ieyasu told them that learning and the military arts should be pursued with equal fervour. In fact, while many *samurai* became teachers of the martial arts others became leading scholars, writers, poets, and artists.

There were occasional upheavals, as, for example, in 1637, when Matsukura Shigeharu, a much-hated *daimyo* ruling the Shimabara peninsula, became so cruel to his people, most of whom were Christian, that he provoked a widespread rebellion. The rebels were surrounded in Hara Castle where they courageously resisted a long siege, forcing the *daimyo* to send for help from the *shogun*. The *shogun's* troops arrived the following year and eventually took the castle, following which they annihilated the rebels and their families, not even the children being spared.

During the Edo era, the *shogunate* was in constant fear of *daimyos* becoming too powerful. Daimyos were regularly accused of rebellious intentions, such an accusation leaving the man concerned with no alternative but to commit *seppuku*, leaving his *samurai* leaderless and transforming them into *ronin*. Since loyalty to one's master was the essence of *bushido*, such *ronin* tried to find a new *daimyo* to serve, but this was frequently difficult; as a result, some were forced to find service as bodyguards for wealthy merchants, while some of the others became rogues or robbers. Indeed, some *samurai* became so poor that they were forced to sell their *katana*, a humiliating and shameful event, which some got around by carrying *tekemitsu*, an imitation sword made of bamboo.

THE COMING OF THE FOREIGNERS

It is almost impossible to appreciate the impact that foreigners have had on Japanese history. First, the Japanese were quite used to dealing with the Chinese and Koreans, but had looked no further and, while their fishermen sometimes sailed great distances, they never produced any great explorers, like the Chinese Admiral Cheng Ho, who could tell at firsthand stories of countries in Southern Asia and the Middle East. Thus, the arrival of Portuguese traders, the first Europeans to visit Japan, landing on an island near Kyushu in about 1543, came as a total

BELOW: The arrival of European traders, shown here on a screen painted in about 1600, had an immense impact. They brought commercial goods, weapons such as muskets, and ideas, such as Christianity, all of which were unsettling.

surprise. Not only were they physically different, but they also brought missionaries as well as trade.

One of the earliest missionaries was Saint Francis Xavier (1506-62), a Spanish Jesuit, who arrived with two companions at Kagoshima in 1549. He studied the Japanese language for a year, following which he preached in many of the principal cities, and by the time he left the country in 1551 had established several small but vigorous Christian communities. As a result of his and other Jesuits' efforts, and, despite official disapproval and persecution by Hideyoshi, by the end of the 16th Century there were some 300,000 Japanese Roman Catholics. In addition, growing numbers of Portuguese, Spanish, and Dutch traders visited the country and the *shogunate* became convinced that Christianity was serving as a preliminary to an all-out conquest by one or other of the European powers.

In 1612 Christians became subject to officially sanctioned persecution, and various massacres followed. In 1624 the Spanish were refused permission to land and further edicts in the next decade prevented Japanese from travelling abroad; even the building of large ships was forbidden. The European presence was reduced to a small group of Dutch traders restricted to the tiny island of Deshima in Nagasaki harbour, with very onerous limitations on their numbers and activities.

THE EMPERORS

Japan is unique among the kingdoms and empires of the world in that it has only ever had a single ruling dynasty, the throne having passed from one member to another of the same family from pre-historic times onwards. The emperor was thus a figure of almost mystical significance to his people and even though many were mere puppets, all provided the essential symbol of national continuity. The person of the emperor, what power he was able to exercise, and who was likely to be the next emperor were matters of grave concern throughout the *samurai* period. One matter of particular importance was that all official acts were done in the emperor's name.

From the beginning of the Japanese empire until approximately a hundred years after the introduction of Buddhism and the growth of a Chinese-style official class, the emperor was the actual ruler, with no artificial barrier placed between him and his people. Thereafter, however, he became increasingly cut off until, as will be described, he was to all intents and purposes totally isolated.

Apart from having the blood royal running in his veins, it was essential that the emperor possessed the three items of the sacred regalia. Japanese *Shinto* traditions hold that the first manifestation of maleness (*izanagi*) and femaleness (*izanami*) produced a number of children, although there are several different versions of what happened next. According to one of the most popular, they had five children: *Amaterasu*, the eldest, who became the Sun-Goddess; Tsuki, the Moon Goddess; Hiruko, a cripple, who became the God of Seas and Storms; Sosanoo, a very badly behaved boy; and a third son, who became the God of Wild Fire. It was during this period that the three sacred emblems were created: a mirror, which was given to Amaterasu to enable her to see herself; a sword, named "Cloud Cluster" which Sosanoo found in a dragon he had slain and presented to Amaterasu; and a stone seal. Amaterasu's son, Ninigi-no-Mikoto, descended to Earth, carrying these objects and arrived on the summit of Mount Kirishima in Japan According to the tradition, his great-grandson, Jimmu Tenno, became the first emperor of Japan.

The line of descent of the emperors has been very carefully catalogued in an official list, the first of which was compiled during the reign of Temmu (40). This list begins with Jimmu (1), which was officially reaffirmed in 1873, when it was stated that detailed research had established his date of accession as February 11 660 BC (using the dates of the Christian calendar). Since the issue of that first list, constant scholarly research has resulted in several amendments, although very little is known about the early emperors; indeed, of those reigning between 549 and about 98 BC, nothing is known apart from their names. However, the research has enabled several amendments to be made, with Kobun (39) being added in 1870 and Chokei (98) in 1923. The list, which is maintained by the Imperial Household Agency, now includes 125 emperors and empresses regnant.

All emperors have married and until very recently they had numerous wives. One, however, was always selected as the principal wife and the title "*koga*" was suffixed to her name.

LEFT: *Access to Japan was forbidden to all except Chinese and Dutch merchants in 1639. The Dutch were confined to Dejima island in Nagasaki harbour (seen here), but contacts with ordinary Japanese were banned.*

BELOW: *The "Conquest of Korea by Empress Jingu" by Sumiyoshi Hiroyuki (1753-1811). The emperors and empressses regnant, such as Jingu, played a vital role in Japanese history and customs, their imperial blood and possession of the ancient symbols providing a sense of national unity and continuity, even though they rarely exercised real power.*

For many centuries it was possible for there to be an empress regnant, the first on the official list being Suiko (33). However, this was officially discontinued by the Imperial Household Law of 1889, which restricts the succession to males only, making Go-Sakuramachi (117) the last of the empresses regnant.

There are some surprising exclusions from the list, including Himiko, the warrior queen, who, according to Chinese histories, ruled Yamataikoku in the 3rd Century AD. Nor does the Empress Jingu appear in the list, even though it seems reasonably certain that she ruled from the death of her husband, Emperor Chuai (14), in 200 AD until the accession of their son, Ojin (15) in 260 AD.

Descent was frequently in a direct line from one emperor to his eldest son, but this was by no means always the case. If the eldest was considered unsuitable, a younger brother or nephew of the incumbent could be declared the heir, or sometimes even a descendant of an earlier emperor, while in earlier times the throne was sometimes taken by force (eg, Temmu (40) from Kobun (39) in 672) but always with the qualification of the blood royal. Who made the choice was also often a problem. Sometimes it was the incumbent emperor himself, but, especially in the case of a young emperor, the choice could be made by the "cloistered emperor" or even when there was more than one ex-emperor living, by the most senior of them. There were also cases where the chief minister or, later, the *bukafu* made the choice.

In earlier times, emperors were mature at the time of their accession, but in 683 AD Mommu (42) became the first minor to accede, being only 14 years of age at the time. There were many more minors later, however some acceding at age two or three. Such youngsters were, not unnaturally, under the domination of adults, either the regent, the most senior of the "cloistered emperors," or the *shogun*.

Emperors rarely died in their beds during their reign. Some were assassinated, such as Sushun (32) who was killed in 592, many abdicated either voluntarily or were forced into doing so, while one, Antoku (81), died at the Battle of Dan-no-ura, but as a seven-year old and in the arms of his grandmother.

The imperial schism which lasted from 1337 to 1392 started with a row between Emperor Go-Daigo (96) and the *shogunate*, which culminated in the emperor fleeing the capital in 1331, taking the sacred regalia with him, which he then hid. He was caught, but having refused to divulge the whereabouts of the regalia, he was exiled to an island in the Sea of Japan. In a confused series of events Go-Daigo regained power but was then forced to flee again in 1337 and established his own court at a Buddhist temple at Yoshino, thus beginning the split.

From then on there were two courts. The "Northern Court" was at Kyoto, presided over by emperors of the Jimyo-In branch of the imperial family: Kogon (North 1) and his descendants. The *shogunate* was also at Kyoto. The Southern Court was at Yoshino under the "Southern emperor": Go-Daigo (96) and his descendants. Both sets of emperors were of the imperial blood, but those at Yoshino possessed the regalia.

The rift was eventually healed by negotiation, culminating in the Southern emperor, Go-Kameyama (99), making a formal progress to Kyoto where, under the terms of the agreement, he immediately abdicated, handing over the regalia to Go-Komatsu (100). Because the Southern emperors had retained the regalia they are shown as the official line, but the "Northern emperors" are included in the table for completeness, and, in any case, it was from them that the line then continued.

For most of their existence, the emperors passed their time in delicate and refined idleness, their interests engaged in intellectual, artistic, religious, philosophical, and amorous matters. One brief story will illustrate the atmosphere in which the court lived and concerns Seisho Nagon, an imperial concubine, who was particularly well-versed in Chinese and Japanese literature. One morning, at the usual assembly of the lords and ladies of the court, the emperor enquired, referring to a nearby mountain: "How is the snow of Kuroho?" Seisho Nagon immediately lifted the curtain to reveal the mountains covered in newly fallen snow. She alone among those present had grasped the emperor's allusion to an ancient but obscure Japanese poem, which contained the line, "The snow of Kuroho is seen by raising the curtain." The emperor duly rewarded her for her knowledge and perspicacity. However, life outside such refined circles was considerably more violent and vulgar. Indeed, for many at the court, the only signs of real animation seem to have come where matters of their own safety or court protocol were concerned. In this life of empty pomp and idle luxury, the emperors were surrounded by a seemingly impenetrable wall of etiquette that isolated them from the outer world. They never appeared in public and, with the exception of wives, consorts and the highest ministers, no-one ever saw their faces. The emperor's feet were never allowed to touch the earth and when he travelled it was in a carriage drawn by bullocks and was closely curtained. Not surprisingly, such secluded beings became the very stuff of mythology.

In the 16th Century the imperial court became so impoverished that Go-Tsuchimikado (103) and his successor Go-Kashiwabara (104) could not afford to abdicate, and even the ceremonies surrounding the unavoidable events such as burials were strictly curtailed. The accession ceremony, which had three stages, had to be spread over a long period in order to make it affordable, and the full ceremonies were not totally revived until the accession of Empress Meisho in 1629. Go-Nara (105) was so impoverished that he was forced to supplement his tiny official income by writing and copying poems on commission, and by selling his autograph. Go-Toba (82) became a swordsmith of some distinction, although this was mainly in pursuit of his goal of regaining the throne.

As was inevitable, the behaviour of some emperors was less than perfect. Occasionally, a streak of violence and cruelty emerged, in particular with Buretsu (25), Yozei (57) and Shoko (101). Anko (20), murdered his father in order to gain the throne, while Yuryaku (21) arranged the murder of all possible alternative candidates to ensure his succession.

In all, 58 emperors and empresses regnant have abdicated, the first to do so being Keitai (26) in 531 AD, who was ill, and the next Empress Kogyoku (35) in 642 AD. Some emperors and empresses were put on the throne when the intended successor was too young and there was a strict understanding that they would abdicate as soon as the real successor had reached a reasonable age. Many emperors who abdicated continued to exercise a strong hold over imperial family matters, being known as *Ho-o* ("cloistered emperor)."

All emperors married and had numerous wives, many of them begetting a whole host of children, some as many as 50. This caused severe problems and from time to time emperors tried to contain the ever-proliferating ranks of the nobility. Emperor Saga (52), for example, had some 50 offspring and their support in imperial style became such a burden that he deprived the seventh and subsequent sons of their imperial status. Instead, he declared them to be ordinary subjects, giving them the new clan name of Minamoto, a name which was to reappear later in Japanese history. This ruling did not, however, prove to be absolute and with other claimants being unsuitable Minamoto Sadami, seventh son of Koko (58), had his imperial status restored in order that he could inaugurated as crown prince on the day before his father died, acceding to the throne as Uda (59).

An earlier emperor, Ingyo (19), demanded that some with dubious claims to nobility should prove their rights. He declared that true nobles would miraculously withstand submerging their arms in boiling water or mud and invited those with suspect rights to noble titles to prove their nobility in this manner. Not surprisingly, many titles were allowed to lapse rather than submit to such a trial.

ABOVE: The Emperor Go-Toba, who reigned from 1183-1198, became a noted swordsmith, a highly respected activity in a society that lived by the sword. This print by Kuniyosghi shows him beating a sword blade on an anvil, with the Fox-spirit assisting him in the background.

Chapter 2

SAMURAI WARFARE

Until the early 15th Century, a Japanese battle usually started with the two sides facing each other, following which individuals would step forward out of the ranks and issue challenges to single combat. This involved a loud declamation of the challenger's pedigree, glorifying his ancestors and their martial deeds, and ending with his own. Eventually this challenge would be accepted and the two men would then start their combats mounted and using bows and arrows. If this failed to achieve an outcome they would close and attack each other with swords or even come to grips with each other and try to despatch their opponent with a dagger. The aim of such individual engagements was to end up with the enemy's head.

This procedure held good provided that both sides understood the significance of the challenge, comprehended the language, and were prepared to follow the rules. In other words, both sides had to be Japanese, which was not the case during the first Mongol invasion in 1274, when a *samurai* army met the Chinese invaders on the shore of Hakata Bay. When individual Japanese warriors came forward and started declaiming loudly in an incomprehensible language, the Mongols, who had no idea what their enemy was up to, simply swept forward, engulfing the would-be champions in order to attack the main body of their enemy.

SAMURAI ARMIES

From the early 15th Century onwards, however, the *samurai* armies became much better organized. They deployed and manoeuvered for advantage, and fought as a body, although individual combats still occasionally took place. These armies were made up of three elements: *samurai*, of which there were two types, mounted and unmounted; *ashigaru*, who were foot soldiers; and porters and other support troops.

SAMURAI

All cavalrymen were *samurai* and in the earlier part of the period their main weapon was the bow, although they later came to be armed with the *mochi-yari*, a spear some 13 feet (4 m) long. In attacking other cavalry, the rider could either sit down in his saddle and use the spear as a piercing weapon, or he could stand in his stirrups and use the spear blade to slash at his opponent, which was not particularly difficult, since the spear was not very heavy. Against *ashigaru* or dismounted *samurai*, the cavalryman could use either the spear or the sword and, of course, the momentum of the horse itself. Most *samurai* fought on foot, when their main weapon was the spear, and many peacetime hours were spent in practising the art of fighting against opponents armed with either spears or swords.

ASHIGARU

The *ashigaru* (= light foot) were originally peasant farmers, whose normal occupation was tilling the soil, but who became soldiers when ordered to do so by their *daimyo*. Gradually, however, they became full-time soldiers. Some of the *ashigaru* were employed in roles roughly equivalent to that of a European squire, providing personal attendants to senior officers, as well as drummers, flag-bearers, and so on. But the vast majority were infantry, who became increasingly specialized, the main divisions being into pikemen, archers, and arquebusiers. The number of men in each unit varied from one *daimyo* to another, but they were generally divided into platoons of approximately 30 men each. In some platoons all men carried the same weapon, but others were organized into mixed platoons of arquebusiers and archers. Such units included integral porters, equipped with special carrying-frames, each containing 100 arrows for instant resupply of the archers.

The commander of the *ashigaru* was a *samurai*, the *ashigaru taisho*. Further, since *ashigaru* seem to have been considered stupid and mule-like, their units had a high proportion of officers, all of them *samurai*, who exercised tight and detailed control, especially over the expenditure of arrows and bullets.

LOGISTICS

Samurai armies were frequently up to 50,000 strong and logistic support for such a force was not a matter to be treated lightly. The baggage train consisted of large numbers of pack horses, carts drawn by men or oxen, and porters, which were collectively responsible for carrying weapons, ammunition, equipment, rations for the men, fodder for the horses, and the other necessities of campaigning. The baggage train was manned by peasants (*chugen*), who served as carriers, labourers, grooms, and so on. Numerous *samurai* were involved in the command and control of this body, which may not have been the most glamorous job for an ambitious warrior, but was one which, if done badly or carelessly, could have disastrous repercussions for the whole force.

COMMAND AND CONTROL

An army was commanded by a general who, by tradition, would sit on a stool on a high spot, from where he could survey the battlefield. His position was identified by a screen (*maku*) and a large banner. Among the groups of attendants surrounding him were the *tsukai*, a group of *samurai*, specializing as messengers, who wore special distinguishing marks, a system closely analogous to aides-de-camp in a pre-modern European army.

BELOW: A mounted samurai charges into battle. Note the bow, arrows, armour, leopard-skin saddle-cloth and heavily decorated stirrups.

HERALDRY

Japanese battlefield heraldry was based on the *mon* (family device), of which there were large numbers, varying from stylized flowers or insects, through one or more written characters, to scenic paintings.. At the highest level, there were two imperial seals or badges: one for palace and family business, consisting of a flower and leaves of the *paulownia imperialis* (*kiri*), the other for external, public business, which was a chrysanthemum (*kiku*).

At the next level, the Tokugawa family crest (and that of their *shogunate*) was a circle enclosing three inward-facing leaves of the *awoi* plant (a species of holly-hock). Among the principal families, the devices included: Maeda family — five circles with ten short rays symbolizing sword wounds; Kuroda — black disk; Hosokawa — a small disk surrounded by eight larger disks; Mori — a water-plant. Hideyoshi took a slightly different approach, adopting the gourd as his symbol and then adding one further gourd for each battle he won.

Such *mon* were painted on the various displays found on the battlefield, and were essential for recognition of friend and foe. The senior general on the battlefield displayed a long banner, suspended from its top edge, known as the *o uma jirushi* (great standard). His headquarters was also partially surrounded by a large screen (*maku*) upon which his *mon* was displayed.

ABOVE: A display of mon, *the family emblems whose origins lay in the need for leaders to have some means of identification in battle.*

FAR RIGHT: A samurai *dressed for battle was an awe-inspiring sight. His long-range weapon was the bow, which was used for individual duels.*

Each *daimyo* had either a *nabori* or a *fukiniki*. A *nabori* was carried on a pole shaped like an inverted "L," with the flag laced to the top bracket and shaft, so that it was held out, regardless of the wind, enabling its device to be seen clearly at all times. The alternative was a *fukiniki*, a cylindrical streamer, suspended from the top of a long pole. Major units under the *daimyo's* command also carried a *nabori* or *fukiniki*. Carrying such a banner was a sought-after privilege and many lives were expended in trying either to capture or defend such potent symbols.

From the early 16th Century onwards all *samurai* started to carry *sashini*, essentially a smaller version of the *nabori*. It was carried on a short pole on the wearer's back and held upright by two strings which passed under his arm-pits to two rings on his chest, where they were tied-off. Such banners could carry one of a variety of devices, including the *daimyo's mon*, the bearer's *mon*, or, in some cases, simply his name.

Ashigaru wore an iron corselet, which bore the general's *mon*, and even packhorses sometimes carried an identifying flag on a short stick.

These were, however, by no means the only devices to be seen on a *samurai* battlefield. Others included presentation banners (eg, from the emperor), religious banners and a wide variety of symbols. These combined to ensure that a *samurai* battlefield was awash with a profusion of banners and symbols.

TACTICS

APPROACH TO CONTACT

Armies marched and approached each other in column, but then deployed into battle formation. Such formations were commonly used by all Japanese armies, having been developed from those given in Chinese scripts. Individual formations, and the redeployment from one to another, were regularly practised in peacetime.

FIREARMS

Following its introduction in the 16th Century, the arquebus rapidly assumed greater importance on the battlefield. The general concept for its use was for the two sides to have arquebusiers in their respective front ranks and for these to advance to within about 100 yards (90m) of each other (possibly closer) where they halted and then fired in volleys. If one side started to falter the order would be given for the *samurai*, either cavalry or on foot, to pass through and charge.

One major tactical problem was that the slow rate of fire meant that an arquebusier was particularly vulnerable whilst reloading. This was partly overcome by deploying the arquebusiers in two ranks, one firing and the other reloading, and partly by forming mixed groups of archers and arquebusiers, with the former firing while the latter were reloading.

SWORDSMEN

The main weapon of the *samurai* was the sword, which was specifically designed as a slashing and cutting weapon, not for thrusting, as in Europe. Not surprisingly, apart from individual combats at the start of a battle, the main use of the sword was in a general *melee*. Not only *samurai*, but also *ashigaru* archers, arquebusiers, and pikemen had to be prepared to take part in such hand-to-hand combat.

ARCHERS

Until about the beginning of the 16th Century *samurai* always carried bows, which they used for individual duels, but thereafter they were carried only by the *ashigaru*. Such *ashigaru* archers were employed as sharpshooters, with each shot being aimed at a specific target and they do not seem to have been used to produce volleys of arrows, as employed on other continents.

PIKEMEN

Although *samurai* armed with spears used their weapons in individual combat, *ashigaru* pikemen, whose weapon was longer and heavier, employed their pikes collectively, according to a precise drill. In this, the pikemen were dressed off in line, with approximately one arm's length between each man, and then ordered to kneel and lay their pikes on the ground in front of them. When an enemy cavalry charge was imminent the initial aim was to kill horses and to unseat their riders. At the order of their commander, the pikemen would pick up their weapons, place the butt in the scabbard and then brace themselves, with the tips of all spears at the same height as a horse's breast, thus presenting an

obstacle which was very difficult to penetrate. Pikes could also be used offensively, with the pikemen advancing in line, again with their pikes extended and the blades at the same height.

AFTER THE BATTLE

The formalities of the battle were not completed until the victorious side had followed certain rituals, most of which centred upon the taking and inspection of heads of fallen *samurai*. These were carefully collected by those who had vanquished them, and were cleaned, dressed and labelled before being mounted on a small wooden board and offered in turn for inspection by the commanding general. The latter would take note of the dead man's name and status, and would pay particular attention to the expression on the dead man's face. Then, taking note of the nature of the combat in which the dead man had fallen, he would reward the victor accordingly, sometimes with a title, sometimes with gold.

Even on the victorious side there was bound to be a proportion of wounded *samurai* and these were by no means ignored. Surgery was rough and ready, but probably no more so than in contemporary European armies. Thus, an arrow barb could be pulled out by a pair of pincers, while sword cuts were sewed or bound together using tough Japanese paper, of which every soldier carried a supply. This paper was soft but strong, making excellent bandages or tourniquets and it was effective in healing wounds. Acupuncture and the use of natural hot springs were also considered efficacious in healing wounds.

TRAINING

Training was taken very seriously; indeed, during the long peace of the Tokugawa *shogunate*, there was no other way a *samurai* could demonstrate his prowess. In the early 1870s, when many of the traditional customs continued unchanged, an American teacher observed:

"...Six of the students repaired to the armory and put on the defensive mail, to shield themselves in the rough work before them — as Japanese swords are for use with both hands, having double-handed hilts without guards. The foils for fencing are made of round, split-bamboo, and a good blow will make one smart and bruise the flesh. So, the fencing-master and students first donned a corselet, with shoulder-plates of hardened hide padded within, and heavily padded gauntlets. On their heads were wadded caps, having a barred visor of stout iron grating. Taking their places, with swords crossed, they set to. All the passes are cutting blows, thrusting being unknown. Pretty severe whacks are given, and some bruising done, in spite of armor. Foils are used up like lances in a tournament. The young men kept up the mimic battle for 15 minutes, or as long as their wind and muscle lasted, and the severe ordeal was over, the victory being won by those who had given what would have been disabling wounds had swords been used..."

Castles and Siege Warfare

Throughout Japanese history, fortifications and castles have been important military assets, and by the end of the *samurai* period there were many hundreds of castles throughout the country, with one in almost every feudal city and place of strategic importance. Much thought was given to the siting, design, construction, and defence of such fortifications, as well as to the conduct of sieges. Castles were generally sited on tactically significant ground, such as natural hilltops or rocky outcrops, but failing that there was no shortage of peasant labour to "improve" positions — for example, by excavating huge ditches or transporting large stones over long distances.

Design / construction

The design of a Japanese castle (*shiro*) was quite different from that found in Europe and the Middle East. Up to about the beginning of the 16th Century most consisted of an outer palisade surrounding a wide, deep ditch, inside which was a continuous wall constructed of wood and plaster, with loopholes and platforms for the defenders to use their weapons. This wall also included a number of watchtowers and inside were buildings to accommodate the garrison.

When Ieyasu started his great modernization programme, however, the design became much more sophisticated. The outer ditches were made much wider and deeper, and were frequently filled with water to make them into moats. On the inner side of the ditch, the stone walls became much higher and the watchtowers were also higher and more frequent. In many cases a multi-storey central keep was constructed.

Some of these castles — for example, that at Osaka — covered a vast area. Another noteworthy point was the vast size of stones in some of the walls. Osaka Castle, built by Hideyoshi, had stones 40 feet (12m) long, 10 feet (3m) high and 4 feet (1.2m) thick, while those in Tokyo Castle are 16 feet (5 m) long, 6 feet (1.8 m) wide and 3 feet (1m) thick. The latter were brought from near Hyogo, some 200 miles (320km) distant.

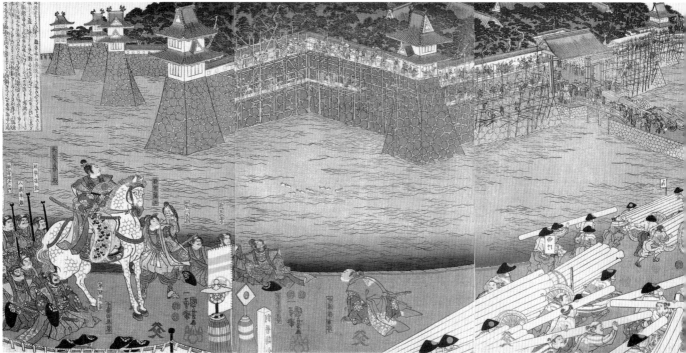

Siege Warfare

The first aim of a besieging force was to surround the castle, in order to cut it off from outside military and logistic support, and then to carry out reconnaissance to discover the layout of the defences, thus identifying weak points in the defence and establishing how they might be exploited. Attempts were usually made to persuade the castellan to give in to a show of overwhelming force, which occasionally succeeded. Failing this, a proper siege had to be started, which might take weeks or even months to succeed.

Such a siege of a major castle was an enormous undertaking. Simply providing an effective force to surround the castle and prevent any moves in or out required large numbers, greatly increased by the need to maintain such a watch around-the-clock. The various siege engines all required large numbers to man, move, and resupply them, while activities such as tunnelling needed large numbers both to do the digging and to remove the spoil. Such a large body of men needed support, which, in turn, required yet more people. This resulted in an army of many thousands, although the largest was probably at the third siege of Odawara Castle in 1590, where Hideyoshi's army numbered some 200,000.

WEAPONS AND SIEGE WARFARE

A variety of defensive weapons were used, including the usual arrows and arquebus. In addition, various objects could be dropped on attackers, including rocks, boiling water, and logs, the latter being held horizontally in nooses until a target was directly below. Many accounts contain references to *samurai* in the besieging force being killed by snipers armed with an arquebus, which suggests that they must have been very close to the enemy.

For the besiegers, a wide variety of devices were developed to protect men working within range of the defender's weapons — for example, when prising stones out of the lower walls. These usually comprised a wooden framework with a solid roof, covered with flameproof animal hides. Most were mounted on wheels and sizes varied according to the number of men to be protected, ranging from the largest type, *kikkosha* (= tortoise wagon), which could accommodate up to a dozen, down to a *komaku*, which protected an individual archer. Siege towers and bamboo ladders of varying sizes were all assembled locally.

Tunnelling was regularly used, employing civil labour, usually professional miners from the many gold, silver, and other mines around the country. The tunnels were dug either to obtain covert access into the citadel or to weaken the foundations of walls and towers, but there were no known instances of using tunnels to place explosives.

Cannon were used to bombard castle walls. The *samurai* armies had their own cannon, which were used in sieges both in their own country and in Korea, but Japanese commanders

LEFT: A samurai *archer on a castle rampart. The bow was asymmetric, the deciduous wood base (usually oak) being covered with a bamboo laminate, which was secured in place by rattan bidings. The bow was also lacquered to make it damp-proof.*

BELOW: An assault party scales the walls of a castle, the lantern indicating that this is being done at night, but the absence of any defenders is rather surprising.

ABOVE: Himeji Castle, showing its dominating position and the series of walls which had to be overcome by the attacker before he could engage the main body of the defenders.

sometimes called on foreign help, one occasion being the long and bloody siege of Hara Castle (1637-1638) which was occupied by the people of the Shimbara peninsula. Matsudaira Nobutsuna (1596-1662), the second commander of the besieging forces (his predecessor had been killed by an arrow), even compelled the Dutch to bring a ship to bombard the castle walls.

Ditches and moats were a problem for the attackers, although they could be overcome. In some sieges, moats were drained and in others ditches were filled in using vast quantities of bundles of green bamboo and rice stalks.

Water supply was most vital for the besieged garrison. Ideally, the castle had its own internal wells, since external supplies were always vulnerable. At the siege of Futamata in 1572, for example, the castle obtained its water by lowering buckets from a special tower into the river. The besieging force, seeing this, floated a succession of rafts down the river which hit the tower's supports in succession, eventually causing the tower to collapse and the garrison was forced to surrender.

Food supply was also essential and starvation always became a problem in a protracted siege, not least because the garrison frequently included a large number of local peasants who had been forced into the fortress by the arrival of the besieging army. Starving out a garrison took a long time, however, and there was always a danger of a relieving army arriving.

THE FATE OF THE DEFEATED

Provided that the siege had not been too long or costly, surrender terms were sometimes bloodless (eg, Shiyama Honganji, 1576-80), although they could also include suicide by the commander, as at Takamatsu (1582). But the usual fate of the defenders of a castle which resisted until it was carried by storm was death, frequently to the last woman and child. When Nobunaga, for example, besieged Nagashima for the third time in 1574, he eventually took it by building a huge pile of brushwood, which

was ignited when the wind was in the correct direction. Sparks and embers were blown inside the fortifications, starting a conflagration in which all 20,000 defenders were consumed. Similarly, when Shimbara Castle fell, some 37,000 defenders were massacred, including several thousands who were forced to jump off a cliff in Nagasaki harbour.

By no means all sieges were successful. A well-sited and well-prepared castle, with adequate food and water, and a determined garrison, could hold out for a long time. A particular problem for the besiegers occurred if a relieving army approached, when the commander of the besieging force found himself caught between two stools.

TREACHERY

Treachery among the besieged garrison sometimes played a role in their defeat. Two examples were Nanao (1577) where a traitor opened the castle gate, and Hiuchi (1183) where a message attached to an arrow told the besiegers where to breach the moat in order to drain it. A more elaborate effort was made by Akechi Mitsuhide (1526-1582) who, when besieging Yagami Castle (1578), sought to end the siege by kidnapping the mother of the commander, Hatano Hideharu, threatening her execution unless her son surrendered. Hideharu duly surrendered, but Mitsuhide's lord, Oda Nobunaga (1534-1582), crucified the mother and beheaded the son. Such behaviour engendered bloody revenge. First, some of Hideharu's former vassals killed Mitsuhide's mother, and two years later Mitsuhide killed Nobunaga.

Apart from traitors, *shinobi* (spies/infiltrators) were also used by both besiegers and besieged to gain intelligence, a role later performed by the *ninja*. Even in peacetime, castellans always ensured that there was the strictest watch at the castle gates and, although visitors were admitted inside the outer walls, no retainer of another *daimyo*, no matter how exalted, was ever allowed into the citadel.

THE SAMURAI HOME

An important *samurai*'s house was permanently guarded by his armed retainers, who had a guard-house beside the gate, with one man on duty and others on call inside. Visitors known to the guards were allowed in and out without challenge, but strangers had always to prove their identity and state the reason for the visit. The guards usually had a variety of weapons at their disposal, including staves and swords.

Chapter 3

FEARSOME WARRIORS

I n its purest form, the term *samurai* describes a type of intellectual warrior, whose closest European parallel might be the Knights Templar, except that the *samurai* were an entire class in society, rather than a small closed society. For many centuries these warriors had an absolute monopoly on the bearing of arms and epitomized the ideas of

BELOW: The early samurai *lived by the code of* kyuba no michi *(way of horse and bow), which was intended to develop "freedom from fear."*

patriotism and devotion to military duty. Conversely, they were also at the forefront of Japan's intellectual development, making great achievements in the fields of literature, the arts and music, and transforming the simple act of drinking tea into a ceremony of the highest artistic significance. As in most fields of human endeavour, however, while the goals were lofty and aspired to by all, only a few men actually attained such perfection. The majority fell slightly short of the ideal, and a few never even approached them.

BUSHIDO

The warriors' code was developed from the Chinese concept of the virtues of warriors doing battle into, first, the *samurai* code of chivalry known as *kyuba no michi* (= Way of Horse and Bow) and, subsequently, into the *bushido* (= Way of the Warrior). The word *samurai*, itself, came from the Japanese root meaning to be on one's guard, or to guard (*saburau*). The *samurai* emerged in the early 10th Century AD, and established themselves as the warrior class, following a special code known as *bushido*. Originally, the term *samurai* covered the whole military system of Japan, both nobles and vassals, but by the beginning of the 12th Century it had come to be specifically applied to the military retainers of a *daimyo*, the feudal barons under the *shogun*. These *samurai* lived under a *bushido*, the code of ethics which was at the heart of their beliefs and conduct. It was intended to provide a philosophical foundation for a "freedom from fear," which would enable a *samurai* to transcend the fear of death, thus giving

BELOW: Minamoto-no-Yoritomo (1147-1199), the son of a samurai, *became the first* Minamoto shogun *in 1185, despite suffering many setbacks both in his personal life and in his military career.*

him the peace and power to serve the *daimyo* (his master) faithfully and loyally, and to die well if necessary. *Bushido* was summarised by one philosopher as:

"I have no parents; I make the Heavens and the Earth my parents.
I have no home; I make the *Tan T'ien* my home.
I have no divine power; I make honesty my Divine Power.
I have no means; I make Docility my means.
I have no magic power; I make personality my Magic Power.
I have neither life nor death; I make *A Um* my Life and Death.

I have no body; I make Stoicism my Body.
I have no eyes; I make The Flash of Lightning my eyes.
I have no ears; I make Sensibility my Ears.
I have no limbs; I make Promptitude my Limbs.
I have no laws; I make Self-Protection my Laws.

I have no strategy; I make the Right to Kill and the Right to Restore Life my Strategy.
I have no designs; I make Seizing the Opportunity by the Forelock my Designs.
I have no miracles; I make Righteous Laws my Miracle.
I have no principles; I make Adaptability to all circumstances my Principle.
I have no tactics; I make Emptiness and Fullness my Tactics.

I have no talent; I make Ready Wit my Talent.
I have no friends; I make my Mind my Friend.
I have no enemy; I make Incautiousness my Enemy.
I have no armour; I make Benevolence my Armour.
I have no castle; I make Immovable Mind my Castle.
I have no sword; I make my Mind my Sword."

The *samurai*'s life was likened to that of the cherry blossom, being beautiful but with a brief life. For the man, as for the flower, early death followed naturally and gloriously as expressed in the *Hagakure* by Yamamoto Tsunetomo:

"The *Way of the Samurai* is found in death and if there are alternatives, there is only the quick choice of death, which is not particularly difficult. To die without reaching one's aim is as meaningless as a dog's death and is the frivolous way of sophisticates. When pressed with the choice of life or death, it is not necessary to gain one's aim; we all want to live and in large part we make our logic according to what we like. But failing to attain our aim whilst carrying on living is the cowardly way. This is the substance of the *Way of the Samurai*. If by setting one's heart right every morning and evening, one is able to live as though one's body were already dead, one gains freedom in the *Way*. In this way the *samurai*'s whole life will be without blame, and he will succeed in his calling."

As in the rules of chivalry prevailing in medieval Europe, *bushido* was based on a series of virtues, which included rectitude, endurance, frugality, courage, politeness, veracity, and, especially, loyalty to one's lord. Only through the exercise of these virtues could a *samurai* maintain his honour, and a failure to live up to any of these high ideals meant that a *samurai* had forfeited his honour and had no choice but to commit *seppuku* (ritual suicide).

The code of *bushido* was fully developed as an oral tradition by the late 12th Century and became a written code in the 16th Century. When feudalism was abolished in the mid-19th Century, the code was formally abandoned, although its influence, mainly within the Japanese armed forces, persisted.

The code was complex and some elements were purely practical, concerning such matters as swordsmanship. The ethical code, however, may be considered to have had two elements: military and social. The military tenets were:

  loyalty to superiors, which transcended all else, including family considerations;
  unquestioning obedience, despite hardships or danger;
  acceptance of death in battle and rejection of escape or surrender;

LEFT: Fukushima Masanori (1561-1624) with his famous spear Nihongo, *which he used at the Battle of Shizugatake (1583), killing Haigo Gozaemon with a single thrust through the armpit. Later, Masanori lost* Nihongo *in a wager and his pleas to keep it are retold in a famous song,* Kurodabushi.

indifference to pain;

The social elements were:

the importance of the family, based on reverence and respect for parents
willingness to sacrifice oneself for family honour;
consideration for the feelings of others;
personal honesty.

Further, if he saw corruption or disloyalty in another, the *samurai* was expected to slay the guilty party and then commit *seppuku*, lest his honourable intentions be questioned.

It was considered a great honour to be a *samurai*, which was officially designated as a caste of the lower nobility. *Samurais* intermarried within their own caste, and all the sons received certain privileges and honours at birth, together with responsibilities, such as *giri*, the *samurai*'s

RIGHT: Minamoto Yoritomo rides into battle at the tender age of thirteen. He went on to fight in many engagements, culminating in the Battle of Dan-no-ura (1185), a sea fight in which the Minamoto decisively defeated the Taira. He became shogun *in 1185.*

responsibility toward his master. Only the legitimate heir, however, received his father's pension. A *samurai* son was trained in etiquette and military arts, and on his seventh birthday he received the *hakama* (= wide trousers), followed by the two swords on his 15th birthday, when he was also permitted to wear his hair in the style of the *samurai*.

In ancient times it was the custom for warriors to wear their hair long and to grow moustaches and beards. During the medieval period, however, it became customary for military men to shave their temples and the middle of their scalps, leaving a long queue which was bound into a top-knot, to ensure that the hair was kept out of the eyes in battle. Such a style was originally that of the warrior although its use gradually extended to other classes.

The *samurai* formed a distinct class, instantly recognizable by the two swords which symbolized their caste. Their continued existence arose out of the endless battles for land among three main clans – the Minamoto, the Fujiwara and the Taira – and the *samurai* eventually achieved their distinctive status between the 9th and 12th Centuries A.D. They were called by two names: *samurai* (knights-retainers) and *bushi* (warriors). Some *samurai* were related to the ruling class and others were hired men, but all gave complete loyalty to their *daimyo*, their role being to protect his land and to extend his rights to more land. In return the *samurai* received land and position.

The last *shogun* resigned in 1867, and the privileges enjoyed by the *samurai* were withdrawn when the whole feudal system was abolished in 1871. The Imperial edict forced the *daimyos* to return their lands to the emperor, and the deeply significant practice of wearing swords was prohibited, although both the nobles and their retainers were granted pensions. Then, in 1878, the names *daimyo* and *samurai* were changed to *kwazoki* (nobility) and *shizoku* (gentry), respectively.

KUSUNOKI MASASHIGÉ

For many Japanese one of the greatest personifications of *samurai* virtues is Kusunoki Masashigé, who lived at the beginning of the 14th Century, dying in 1336. The family was descended from the great-grandson of Emperor Bidatsu (32). the name Kusunoki, which means "camphor" in Japanese, having been taken from a grove of such trees in the family's ancestral estate. Masashigé's mother was desperate for a child and prayed to the god Bishamon to become pregnant; accordingly, when she gave birth to a boy she named him Tamon (the Sanskrit name of the god to whom she had prayed) although it was later changed to Masashigé. In boyhood he proved to be so strong that, according to the historical records, by the age of seven he could throw boys of twice his age, and at the age of 12 he beheaded his first enemy in battle. He was also intellectually very advanced, absorbing himself in both Japanese and Chinese classics.

Kusunoki Masashigé lived at the time of enmity between Emperor Go-Daigo (96) and the Hojo regents, and vowed to devote his life to the restoration of Imperial power. By the early 1330s he was one of the leaders, together with Go-Daigo's eldest son, Prince Morinaga. The first phase of their campaign culminated in Ashikaga Takauiji (1305-1358), a senior general in the Hojo army, suddenly changing sides, something which, despite their oaths of loyalty, was by no means unknown in *samurai* history. Faced with certain defeat, the remaining Hojo leaders

ABOVE: Samurai *achieved their warrior status from the 9th Century onwards, and even when on purely civil duties they wore their two swords.*

ABOVE: Japanese art reached the highest levels during the samurai period. The electrifying effect of this samurai urging his horse to gallop ever faster is achieved with an economy of brush work and a rejection of all but the most vital objects in the background.

committed suicide and Go-Daigo was able to return to his capital in triumph in 1333. Unfortunately, the restored emperor handled the situation ineptly, failing to reward his principal helpers, including the turncoat Ashikaga Takauji, who rebelled and captured the capital, Kyoto. Masashigé, however, remained true to his emperor and drove the rebels out of Kyoto.

After this, Masashigé's repeated appeals for further troops to follow up his success fell on deaf ears, and his plans and advice were repeatedly ignored, especially his proposal that the greatly outnumbered Imperial forces should temporarily withdraw to the mountains where they could wage a guerrilla war. Go-Daigo, however, demanded that a stand be made and Masashigé was so loyal that he agreed. As a direct result, when Ashikaga Takauiji counter-attacked Mashahigé was heavily outnumbered and surrounded at the Battle of Minatogawa (1336) and with defeat staring him in the face and convinced that he had done everything which his position enabled him to do, he saw no value in prolonging his life in such a dishonourable situation. So, he went to a farmer's house in the nearby village of Sakurai where, with 16 relatives, he committed suicide. He is still honoured as a shining example of the purity of patriotism, staunchness in devotion to duty, and courage, even in defeat.

SUICIDE

One of the most widely known – and probably also the most misunderstood – aspects of the *samurai* way of life is that of ritual suicide, *seppuko*. At its most basic, the reason for such an act was that the overriding factor in a *samurai*'s life was his military reputation and if he, in any way or on any occasion, failed to act in such a way as to enhance it, especially in battle, then his life was, quite literally, not worth living.

This seems to have originated with the idea that vanquished warriors, especially if they were wounded, would use the shorter of their two swords, either driving them through their chest or mouth, or cutting their throats. This developed into the idea that any defeated warrior, where the position appeared hopeless, would commit suicide and then that the followers of a leader who had committed suicide were bound to follow him. The first, fully authenticated example of *seppuku* is that of Minamoto Tametomo (1139-70), one of the most famous bowmen in *samurai* history, who disembowelled himself after losing a battle.

There were various methods of committing suicide. The most formal, and one unique to the *samurai*, was to use a dagger to slice into the abdomen, which was intended not only to release the spirits, but to do so in the most painful – and thus heroic – way possible. This practice had two names, *seppuku* and *hara-kiri*, which meant the same thing, but the former was a more refined expression, which can be roughly translated as "disembowelment" while the latter was more vulgar, approximating to "belly slitting." At its most formal, this involved the person kneeling down, freeing his jacket to the waist and tucking the sleeves under his knees in such a way that it prevented him from falling forward. He then took his short sword, which was razor sharp, and plunged it into the left side of his stomach, pulled it across to the right, and then gave a slight upwards twist. Originally, the victim would then await his death in very considerable agony, but this was later modified by the presence of a "second," who would watch the principal carry out the ritual disembowellment and then stretch out his neck as a signal to the second to cut off his head. During later times, especially the Tokugawa *shogunate*, it became acceptable for the victim to simply scratch himself in the required pattern with the short sword, prior to stretching out his neck for the second.

However, there were many other methods of committing ritual suicide, including starving oneself to death, burial alive, jumping headfirst from a horse with a sword in one's mouth, jumping off a cliff and deliberately making a solo foray into the midst of the enemy forces.

It was generally accepted that there were a variety of situations in which this could take place, of which a number were not voluntary:

As an "honourable" alternative to execution, when a *samurai* would be "invited" to commit suicide, which was introduced during the Tokugawa *shogunate*.
As a condition of a peace treaty where part of the price paid by the losing side was that either a *daimyo* or a distinguished vassal should commit *seppuku*.

In other situations the *samurai* made the decision himself, particularly in battle to expiate personal failure. This was known as *sokotsu-shi*, and more often than not it was carried out by generals whose battle plan had failed to secure victory. Another reason was to avoid captivity, since from the earliest times the Japanese regarded capture in battle to be singularly demeaning and contemptible, and suicide was the accepted and honourable way to avoid this. In any case, those captured could expect little but bad treatment.

Joining one's lord in death, even a peaceful one, was known as *junshi* and could either precede or follow the master's demise, the aim being to demonstrate that the follower could serve no other master. This practice was repeatedly criticized as being wasteful, especially where the master had died peacefully, and was formally banned on a number of occasions. One of the later examples occurred on the death of Ieyasu's son, Tokugawa Tadayashi (1580-1607), on whose death five of his retainers disemboweled themselves.

A senior retainer could sometimes commit suicide as a desperate bid to protest at the bad behaviour of a superior, when all other forms of counselling had failed. This was known as *kanshi* and was a rare method of criticism, which was sometimes effective, sometimes not. One of the successful cases was that of Hirade Kiyohide, whose 15-year-old master, Oda Nobunaga (1534-1582), proved to be very remiss in ruling the territories under his control. After repeated, but totally ineffective remonstrations, Hirade set out his reasons in a letter and then committed *seppuku*, an action which brought the much-shaken lord to his senses. On the other hand, some cases were ineffectual, as when the last *shogun*, Tokugawa Keiki, lost a series of engagements against the forces loyal to the emperor in early 1868 and all appeared lost. He was advised by one of his ministers to commit suicide to preserve the honour of the Tokugawa clan. But when Keiki refused to do so, the minister himself committed *seppuku*.

Samurai wives occasionally either committed suicide or encouraged their husbands to kill them before the *samurais* themselves commited *seppuku*. For example, in 1583 Shibata Katsutoyo (1530-1583), having suffered several defeats at the hands of Hideyoshi, withdrew to Fukui, where he was soon surrounded and totally cut off. Seeing that his position was hopeless, he gave a grand feast for his family and followers and, when drinking the final toast, told his wife that she was free to escape and to re-marry. She declined, declaring that she would rather join her husband in death, so the men of the doomed garrison then ritually killed their wives and children before themselves committing *seppuku*.

An eyewitness account

In 1868 a group of European officials were allowed to witness a *samurai* commit *seppuku* and one of them has left a graphic description of the event. The event happened as a result of the upheavals in 1868 when the *samurai* concerned had ordered a Japanese artillery battery to fire on the foreign cantonment at Hiogo, causing some casualties. There had been several previous incidents and the foreigners made vehement protests to the imperial court demanding exemplary action, as a result of which an order was issued that the officer who had issued the instruction, Taki Zenzaburo, was to commit *seppuku* to atone for his crime. Representatives of the foreign delegations involved were invited to attend as witnesses, one of whom was a Mr Mitford, secretary to the British consulate. The event took place at 10.30pm in a temple in

Hiogo in the presence of 14 witnesses, seven Westerners and seven Japanese. In the words of Mr Mitford:

"After an interval of a few minutes of anxious suspense, Taki Zenzaburo, a stalwart man, thirty-two years of age, with a noble air, walked into the hall attired in his dress of ceremony, with the peculiar hempen-cloth wings which are worn on great occasion. He was accompanied by a *kaishaku* and three officers, who wore the *jimbaori* or war surcoat with gold-tissue facings. The word *kaishaku*, it should be observed, is one to which our word 'executioner' is no equivalent term. The office is that of a gentleman: in many cases it is performed by a kinsman or friend of the condemned, and the relation between them is rather that of principal and second than that of victim and executioner. In this instance the *kaishaku* was a pupil of Taki Zenzaburo, and was selected by the friends of the latter from among their own number for his skill in swordsmanship.

"With the *kaishaku* on his left hand, Taki Zenzaburo advanced slowly towards the Japanese witnesses, and the two bowed before them, then drawing near to the foreigners they saluted us in the same way, perhaps even with more deference: in each case the salutation was ceremoniously returned. Slowly, and with great dignity, the condemned man mounted on to the raised floor, prostrated himself before the high altar twice, and seated himself on the felt carpet with his back to the high altar, the *kaishaku* crouching on his left-hand side. One of the three attendants then came forward, bearing a stand of the kind used in temples for offerings, on which, wrapped in paper, lay the *wakizashi*, the short sword or dirk of the Japanese, nine inches and a half in length, with a point and edge as sharp as a razor's. This he handed, prostrating himself, to the condemned man, who received it reverently, raising it to his head with both hands, and placed it in front of himself.

"After another profound obeisance, Taki Zenzaburo, in a voice which betrayed so

BELOW: *The picture "The Tale of the Woodcutter" by an anonymous 10th Century artist, shows contemporary Japanese life, with the women of the court in one group and the male warriors in another, while the bowyer pursues his lonely craft, making the bows upon which the others depend.*

much emotion and hesitation as might be expected from a man who is making a painful confession, but with no sign of either in his face or manner, spoke as follows:

'I, and I alone, unwarrantably gave the order to fire on the foreigners at Kobe, and again as they tried to escape. For this crime I disembowel myself, and I beg you who are present to do me the honour of witnessing the act.'

"Bowing once more, the speaker allowed his upper garments to slip down to his girdle, and remained naked to the waist. Carefully, according to custom, he tucked his sleeves under his knees to prevent himself from falling backwards. Deliberately, with a steady hand, he took the dirk that lay before him; he looked at it wistfully, almost affectionately; for a moment seemed to collect his thoughts for the last time, and then, stabbing himself deeply below the waist on the left-hand side, he drew the dirk slowly across to the right-hand side, and, turning it in the wound, gave a slight cut upwards. During this sickeningly painful operation he never moved a muscle of his face. When he drew out the dirk, he leaned forward and stretched out his neck; an expression of pain for the first time crossed his face, but he uttered no sound. At that moment the

kaishaku, who, still crouching by his side, had been keenly watching his every movement, sprang to his feet, poised his sword for a second in the air; there was a flash, a heavy, ugly thud, a crashing fall; with one blow the head had been severed from the body.

"A dead silence followed, broken only by the hideous noise of the blood throbbing out of the inert heap before us, which but a moment before had been a brave and chivalrous man. It was horrible."

["Tales of Old Japan," Volume 1; AB Mitford, MacMillan, London, 1871, pp 232-236.]

RONIN

The most important single element of *bushido* was loyalty to one's lord and so a *samurai* without a master became a contradiction in terms and was placed in a special category known as *ronin* (literally = wavemen). Normally, when a lord died in the normal course of events and had a properly designated heir, then his *samurais'* allegiance transferred automatically to the successor.

But problems arose if the circumstances were different. For example, if the lord fell foul of the government and his property was sequestrated, then the title disappeared. This particularly applied during the Edo period, when the *shogunate* was in permanent anxiety that the *daimyos* would rebel. As a result, they regularly accused the *daimyo* of disloyalty which left the man concerned little option but to commit *seppuku*, thus leaving his followers masterless. On other occasions, a few *samurai* might survive a slaughter in which the majority of their clan had been killed in battle. It was also not unknown for *samurai* to be dismissed.

When *samurai* became *ronin*, they had perforce to seek new lords. Sometimes, for example, in the civil war period, this was not too difficult, but at other times, and especially in the Edo period, it became very difficult indeed. The best managed to find employment with new masters with relative ease. Some formed bands of mercenaries which were hired for a particular campaign; some managed to sink their pride and find employment as rich merchants' bodyguards; but the less fortunate became rogues or robbers and these became a great nuisance. Indeed, some *ronin* became so poor that they sold their *katana*, the worst shame that could befall a self-respecting *samurai* and replaced it with an imitation sword made of bamboo, called *takemitsu*.

CHISHUNGURA: THE FORTY-SEVEN RONIN

One of the most telling and certainly the most popular illustration of loyalty to one's master is a historical event known throughout Japan as the "Forty-seven *Ronin*." This has been immortalized in books, operas and films as *Chishungura* (= treasury of loyal hearts). The series of events started in 1701, at a time when Tokugawa Tsunayoshi was *shogun*, and concerned a *daimyo*, Baron Asano, and his *samurais*. Asano was a member of a very distinguished family: one predecessor, Asano Nagamasa (1546-1610), fought under Toyotomo Hideyoshi; another, Asano Yukinaga (1576-1613), served in the Korean campaign; and yet another, Asano Nagakira (1586-1632) took part in the taking of Osaka Castle. The family fiefdom was in the province of Ako and included what is now the city of Hiroshima.

The Tokugawa *shoguns* imposed many rules to keep the *daimyos* in their place, one of which was that a carefully selected few of this elite had to take it in turn to make all the

arrangements for receiving and entertaining the emperor's envoys sent from the imperial court to visit the *shogun*. This demanded scrupulous attention to detail and carried with it, most conveniently for the *shogun*, meeting all the accompanying expenses. Each of many ceremonies in such an event involved the most minute attention to detail, to ensure that all the demands of protocol and tradition were met, and when Baron Asano was informed of a forthcoming visit he requested and was granted the advice of one of the *shogun's* chiefs of protocol, a man called Kira.

Unfortunately, relations between Asano and Kira rapidly turned very sour. The actual reason has never been discovered, but it may have been that Kira was too openly condescending to a person whom he considered to a be a country chief, or that Kira expected payments which Asano was either not aware of or was not prepared to make. Whatever the problem, Asano took an intense dislike to Kira and one morning, when the two men were in the *shogun's* palace discussing the forthcoming visit, something Kira did or said so infuriated Asano that he suddenly drew his sword and attacked Kira, striking heavy blows on his forehead and shoulder.

Asano's offence was two-fold: first, that he had attacked Kira, but, secondly and much more serious, was that he had drawn his sword in the *shogun's* palace. The outcome was swift, and that afternoon Asano received a delegation of officials from the *shogunate* who told him that he was required to commit *seppuku* at once. A dais of mats was duly assembled and that evening Asano carried out the act according to the prescribed rituals, and the *shogunate* arranged for his body to be taken away and buried at a nearby temple.

News of these events arrived in Ako like a thunderbolt and the dead *daimyo's* retainers considered a variety of steps, ranging from mass suicide to travelling to Edo immediately in order to find and kill Kira. Eventually, they decided to wait for more information and to concentrate their efforts on persuading the *shogunate* that instead of confiscating the Ako domain, as, by custom, it was entitled to do, it should instead allow Asano's younger brother to succeed to the title and lands (and thus, of course, give the *samurai* a new master).

The *shogun* took over a year to reach a decision on what to do, but when he did, it was to confiscate Ako, thus depriving Asano's son of his title and, therefore, transforming the retainers from *samurai* into masterless *ronin*. Infuriated by this and considering that they had nothing further to lose, 47 of Asano's former retainers swore revenge, but they devised a subtle and long-term plan. This involved them giving everyone the impression that, as far as they were concerned, the matter was closed and that they would now just enjoy life — indeed, one of the leaders, Oishi Kuranosuke, deserted his wife and children and lived a life of open dissipation.

The conspirators were, however, merely biding their time and in December 1702 they unobtrusively made their way to the capital, where their promised revenge took place on December 14 1702. They managed to assemble without being noticed and then the "Forty-seven *Ronin*" broke into Kira's house, where they found their victim and his grandson hiding, somewhat ingloriously, in the coal-shed. They contemptuously ignored the younger one, but killed their intended victim and in accordance with the tradition of the Japanese vendetta, they decapitated him and took the head to the temple, where they placed it on their dead master's grave. All the requirements of their oath now being complete, they quietly surrendered to the authorities.

There was immediate and widespread public support for the "Forty-seven *Ronin*" who had demonstrated such intense loyalty to their dead master. Nevertheless, the *shogunate* considered that they had breached the law and ordered them to commit *seppuku*, which they did. Curiously, the *shogun* also ordered the Kira family property to be seized because, during the attack by the *ronin*, Kira's grandson had failed to fight to the death in defending his grandfather.

ASHIGARU

As in Europe, for a long time the *samurai* were the central players in all battles, but the role of the *ashigaru* (= infantry) gradually assumed ever greater importance. Initially, these were simply peasants who were taken on for the duration of a campaign and then released, and their weapons were spears. They were considered to be very inferior in every way to *samurai* — not only socially, but also in their capability as warriors — and played a very subsidiary role on the battlefield. By the 16th Century many *ashigaru* were armed with bows — previously the

LEFT: *Under the leadership of one of their number, Oishi Yoshio, the "Forty-seven* Ronin*" break into Kira's house. They found him hiding in the coal-shed, killed him and then decapitated him, so that they could take his head to the temple and place it on their dead master's grave. Then, their obligations under the code of vengeance complete, they quietly surrendered to the authorities.*

ABOVE: *A* samurai *army on the march at the time of the Gempei Wars. Of particular interest is the wide variety of shafted weapons carried. The iron heads include straight blades, serrated blades, right-angle blades (for hamstringing horses) and axes, all of which would have had a grim effect upon an enemy!*

jealously protected province of the *samurai* — the *ashigaru*s were also allocated the arquebus when this was was introduced from the 1560s onwards. By the time of Tokegawa Ieyasu the *ashigaru* had become full-time professional soldiers — and their status had been raised from the top of the peasantry to the bottom of the *samurai*.

NINJA

Apart from *samurai* and *ashigaru*, there was a third and much more sinister element on the battlefield: the *ninja*. These spies and infiltrators (the modern term would be "special forces") were originally known as *shinobi* and were used by all sides, but especially in sieges where their role was to gain intelligence. The *ninja* were a very secretive group, whose weapons and methods are described separately.

FOUR SAMURAI

Four *samurai* from the middle of the period represent many of the strengths and weaknesses of the system. Oda Nobunaga (1534-1582), Toyotomi Hideyoshi (1537-98) and Tokugawa Ieyasu (1542-1616) were contemporaries. Starting quite separately and from humble origins — in Hideyoshi's case from a peasant family — they worked their way up through the ranks of the *samurai* to become commanders of armies and then unifiers and rulers of Japan. The first was Nobunaga who laid the foundations upon which Hideyoshi built and the third was Ieyasu, who continued the work of both his predecessors and went on to found the Tokugawa *shogunate*, which ruled Japan from 1603 to 1868. The fourth of these *samurai* was a total outsider — a foreigner — who was absorbed into the system with complete success.

ODA NOBUNAGA

Oda Nobunaga (1534-1582) was the son of a minor *samurai* and on his father's death in 1549 he initially showed little inclination to administer the territories he had inherited, leading a life of some dissipation and ignoring the advice of his senior counsellors. Eventually, one of these men, Hirade Kiyohide, committed suicide in order to bring his master to his senses, and his act actually succeeded in doing so. In a complete *volte face*, Nobunaga then set himself the goal of reuniting Japan, which he then pursued relentlessly for the remainder of his life.

Nobunaga slowly expanded his territories but his greatest victory came in 1560 when another *daimyo*, Imagawa Yoshimoto (1519-1560), with an army of some 25,000, attempted to pass though Nobunaga's territory on his way to attack Kyoto. On learning that Imagawa was camping in his territory, Nobunaga set off with an army numbering only 3,000 men and found the enemy army bivouacked in a valley, where they were celebrating recent victories and were less than fully alert. As happened at various times in Japanese history, the weather then came to Nobunaga's aid and a violent thunderstorm forced Imagawa's men to take shelter, which enabled Nobunaga's men to approach undetected. As soon as the storm ended Nobunaga and his men attacked, taking their enemy completely by surprise and routing them and killing Imagawa.

Nobunaga then went from strength to strength in pursuit of his goal of reunification, winning major battles at Inabayama (1564) and Anegawa (1570). One of his major achievements concerned the reduction of the thousand-year-old Buddhist monastery on Mount Hiei. He had realised, quite correctly, that this monastery was far too powerful and exerted too great an influence on both political and military affairs, so he not only totally destroyed the buildings, but ensured that every last monk was found and killed, no matter what their age or involvement in the monastery's affairs.

He was one of the first Japanese to welcome the Europeans, mainly Portuguese and Dutch, who were beginning to reach his country and was so fascinated by Christianity that he was baptised. He also was quick to see the military application of firearms, which had been imported into Japan for some years, but had been regarded mainly as a curiosity. It was Nobunaga, however, who devised tactics, both offensive and defensive, for their use, and retrained his armies accordingly.

Nobunaga's armies conducted three campaigns against the Ikko-ikki stronghold at Nagashima. The first, in 1571, was a total disaster and the second, in 1573, was little better. By 1574, however, Nobunaga was utterly determined to succeed and he devised a complicated but effective plan. The enemy castle was close to the sea and Nobunaga deployed ships, commanded by Kuki Yoshitaka (1542-1600), which bombarded the fortress from the sea, using cannon. Nobunaga captured the outlying forts and then set fire to the fortress, inside which some 20,000 people died.

Nobunaga was one of many in Japanese history to lose his life through treachery, in this case at the hands of a (hitherto) trusted general, Akechi Mitsuhide (1526-1582). This arose from an incident at a banquet during which Nobunaga, in jovial mood, had tucked Akechi's head under his arm and, saying that it reminded him of a drum, struck it lightly with his fan. This was done in front of others, causing Mitsuhide to feel grossly humiliated and to make a secret vow of revenge. His opportunity came in 1582 when Nobunaga despatched a large number of troops to the campaign in Kyushu, leaving the capital relatively lightly protected. Mitsuhide was one of those ordered to Kyushu and he actually set off, but then wheeled back and surrounded the temple where Nobunaga was residing. Nobunaga was struck by an arrow and, realising what was afoot and that death was inevitable, he set fire to the temple and committed *seppuku*. Mitsuhide then marched to Nijo Castle where he found and killed Nobunaga's son and heir, Oda Nobutada (1557-1582).

Nobunaga died at the relatively early age of forty-eight, his dreams of a unified Japan unrealised. Being of Taira descent he was ineligible for the appointment of *shogun*, although the emperor had granted him the title of *naidaijin* (= inner great minister). The task of reunification then fell to his two successors.

TOYOTOMI HIDEYOSHI

Toyotomi Hideyoshi (1537-98) was born in the village of Nakamura in Owari province, where his father, Yasuke, a former *ashigaru* was a small farmer. Hideyoshi, a cheeky boy

with a monkey-like face, refused to fit into the mould of peasant life and managed to secure a job as a *betto* (= groom) to no less a person than Oda Nobunaga, who, noting the boy's martial spirit, suggested that he should become a soldier. Hideyoshi seized opportunities as they occurred and rose rapidly through the ranks of Nobunaga's army, until at the time of his master's death he was commanding an army against the Prince of Choshiu, who ruled 10 provinces in the west. On hearing of Nobunaga's assassination, Hideyoshi quickly made peace with the Prince of Chosiu and marched his 37,000 troopshapidly to Kyoto, where he found Mitsuhide's 16,000-strong army and defeated him at the major Battle of Yamazaki. Mitsuhide fled the battlefield only to meet an ignominious death at the hands of some bandits.

Hideyoshi now took charge and gradually brought Nobunaga's former followers under his flag, either by negotiation or by defeating them in battle. Following the Battle of Shizugatake in 1583 his only remaining opponent was Tokugawa Ieyasu. They fought each other at Nagatuke (1584), which ended in a draw, following which they signed a truce. They eventually became

friends and Ieyasu married Hideyoshi's sister, while late in his life Hideyoshi arranged for his six-year-old son to become engaged to Ieyasu's grand-daughter.

Hideyoshi proved to be as good an administrator as he was a general. For example, he initiated a programme of land surveys to set a fair basis for the collection of rice taxes and banned the possession of weapons by farmers, organising raids with the aim of confiscating swords. His rule also saw the full blossoming of the Momoyama period in which, among many other things, the tea ceremony became popular among the warrior class.

Hideyoshi was considered the greatest Japanese of his time, and shortly after his death he was made a *Shinto* deity, being given the title *Hokoku* (= wealth of the nation). Following the custom of the time, Hideyoshi had no family name when he began his service under Oda Nobunaga, but by the time of his death he had assumed the family name, Toyotomi (= abundant provider).

Hideyoshi's rule did, however, include a number of contradictions, one of which was that, having risen from the very lowest stratum of society to the top, he then took steps to ensure that nobody would be able to do the same in the future. He did this by making class a permanent status for individuals and their offspring, formalised the status of the *samurai* as a separate class and forbade any non-*samurai* from carrying weapons or armour.

The second contradiction was that, having achieved unprecedented tranquillity at home, Hideyoshi carried out two military adventures into Korea, the first in 1592, the second in 1597. This was an attempt to establish a firm base on the Asian mainland from where he could conquer China, but both projects came to naught and when he died in 1598 these dreams of conquest died with him.

Hideyoshi handed over his posts to his son in 1591 and was given the title *taiko* (from which the modern word, *tycoon*, is derived). He died in 1598 and was buried in Kyoto.

TOKUGAWA IEYASU

Tokugawa Ieyasu (1542-1616) was born at Okasaki in Mikawa province (present-day Aichi prefecture) and for most of his childhood was a hostage of the Imegawa clan and for whom he initially fought against Nobunaga. Later he established himself as a *samurai* in Nobunaga's army and rose through the ranks, being granted lands at Mikawa and Suruga. Hideyoshi moved

LEFT: Toyotomi Hideyoshi was born in Nakamura in Owari province in 1537, where his father, a former ashigaru *(foot soldier), had purchased a small farm. Hideyoshi would not follow the peasant's life and somehow managed to secure the job of* betto *(groom) to Oda Nobunaga.*

BELOW: In the early 17th Century Japan looked outwards: foreigners entered the country and Japanese ships such as this reached ports in the East Indies, the Malayan peninsula and Siam. Each needed a government licence from which they were known as "red seal ships".

Ieyasu to a larger domain with a dilapidated castle at the fishing village of Edo, partly in order to reward him for loyal service and to increase his control over eastern Japan, but also in order to place the increasingly powerful Ieyasu where he could keep an eye on him.

On Nobunaga's death, Hideyoshi and Ieyasu were initially in conflict but, as described above, following a drawn battle they became friends. Ieyasu managed to avoid the two expeditions to Korea and by 1600, two years after Hideyoshi's death, he was firmly established as the most powerful feudal lord in the country, his only rivals being an alliance headed by Ishida Mitsunari (1560-1600). The campaign was essentially a series of attempts by each side to control the two great highways, the *Tokaido* and the *Nakasendo*, and after some complicated manoeuvres Ieyasu defeated his enemies at the Battle of Sekigahara (1600).

Following this success Ieyasu established a new central government in Edo (present-day Tokyo) and was granted the title *shogun* by the emperor. Unlike Nobunaga, son of a minor *samurai*, and Hideyoshi, son of a peasant, Ieyasu was eligible to hold this rank since he had Genji blood. Then, aided by some first-rate advisors, Ieyasu built on the models laid down by Nobunaga and Hideyoshi, producing a system of feudal government that was so stable that it lasted for 250 years. As *shogun*, Ieyasu laid down rules and regulations for the *daimyos*, severely limiting their power, and for their *samurai*, whom he encouraged to pursue scholarly learning in addition to their military skills.

Ieyasu's family illustrate some of the complexities of *samurai* genealogy. Ieyasu was the son of Tokugawa Shiro, who lived in a small village called Mutsudaira, in Mikawa. The family claimed descent from the Emperor Seiwa (56) through the Minamoto family line, which was the reason that Ieyasu was eligible to become *shogun*. Ieyasu had 12 children, of whom three were daughters who were married off to wealthy and influential *daimyos*. The eldest son, Tokugawa Nobuyasu (1559-1579), seems to have gone awry and was charged with treason at the relatively young age of 21; the only possible solution was *seppuku*, which he took.

Lacking a son of his own, Toyotomi Hideyoshi adopted Ieyasu's second son, Hideyasu (1574-1607), at which time the boy was known by his real father's original family name, Mutsudaira. When Hideyoshi was 16, however, one of Hideyoshi's wives gave birth to a son (Toyotomi Hideyori [1593-1615]) and Hideyasu was adopted by another *daimyo*, Yuki Harumoto, which meant that his name changed to Yuki Hideyasu. He fought in numerous campaigns and was present at the Battle of Sekigahara, for which he was rewarded with an extensive estate at Echizen. However, Hideyasu's eldest son, Tadanao (1595-1650), having been brought up under the family name of Yuki, chose to revert to the original name of Mutsudaira as an adult and the Mutsudaira of Echizen were noted for their intense loyalty to the Tokugawa *shogunate* throughout its subsequent history.

Ieyasu's third son, Hidetada (1579-1632), was his father's chosen successor and inherited the title of *shogun* which he held from 1605 to 1622. His wife was a daughter of the *taiko*, Hideyoshi. Ieyasu's fourth son, was originally named Tadayasu but this was later changed to Tadayoshi (1580-1607). He was adopted by Matsudaira Ietada (1547-1582), a *samurai* who fought in all Ieyasu's campaigns. Ieyasu's fifth son, Tokugawa Nobuyoshi (1583-1603), died at the age of 20 whereupon five of his followers committed *junshi* (dying with the master).

The sixth son, Tokugawa Tadateru (1593-1683), was given a large estate but, having been late in arriving for the siege of Osaka Castle, he was dispossessed. Despite this, he appears to have lived to the age of 90, showing unusual longevity for those times.

Ieyasu's seventh, eighth and ninth sons were born when their father was 58, 60 and 61 years old, respectively. Obviously the apples of their father's eye, they were given large and very wealthy estates while still infants. The Tokugawa *shogunate* descended in the direct line from Ieyasu to the sixth occupant, after which it passed to Yoshimune, a descendant of the Kii line. The title then continued in that line until the last *shogun* of all, who was a descendant of the Mito line. Nobody in the Owari line ever succeeded to the title. Ieyasu lived for another 12 years after handing over the *shogunate* to his third son, during which he finally captured Osaka Castle and destroyed the Toyotomi clan. He died peacefully in 1616 at the venerable age of 75, but the *shogunate* he founded in Edo in 1603 lasted for another 260 years, giving Japan an unprecedented period of relative tranquillity.

AN ENGLISH SAMURAI

One of the most unusual characters in the story of the *samurai* is an Englishman, Will Adams, who arrived in Japan in about 1607 and settled near Edo. He was a seaman and

RIGHT: Following his success at the Battle of Sekigahara (October 21 1600), Tokugawa Ieyasu puts into practice the ancient Japanese saying, "After victory, the general tightens his helmet strings." Ieyasu then established a new central government and was appointed hereditary shogun *by Emperor Go-Yozei.*

BELOW: A daimyo *processes to the capital,* Edo, *in obedience to the* shogun*'s policy of* sankin kotai.

trained navigator, and also had a good knowledge of both shipbuilding and mathematics. He was accepted into the local community, but, of greater importance, he met Ieyasu on several occasions. Ieyasu not only took a liking to him but also valued his knowledge and abilities so much that he prevented Adams from leaving Japan. Adams was, however, well treated, being made a *samurai* and given the revenue from the village of Hemi, near modern Yokosuka.

Adams had a wife and daughter in England, but when he realised that he would never leave Japan he married a Japanese lady and by her had a son and daughter. He died in 1620 and was buried on a headland overlooking Edo Bay and a street in Edo — Anjin Cho (Pilot Street) — was named in his honour and an annual ceremony in his memory, held on June 15, was still being held in 1873.

Chapter 4

FEARSOME WEAPONS

T he military outfit of a *samurai* was designed primarily for aggression, enabling him to fight and use his weapons, although his armour also provided a certain degree of protection. The outfit also included features which were intended to strike awe into an enemy as well as to provide recognition for friends.

ARMOUR

W estern armour was always fashioned out of either steel plate with articulated joints, or chain mail. Japanese armour, however, was fundamentally different, being fashioned from a large number of small, thin scales, which were fabricated from iron, steel, hardened hide, paper, brass or shark skin, all heavily coated in a thick lacquer. These were fastened together in such a way that the outfit as a whole was strong enough to provide a good degree of protection but sufficiently flexible to enable the wearer to move and to fight.

There were, of course, different styles of armour. In some the *samurai* wore a tunic built up on the lamellar principle, as just described, while in others he wore a solid cuirass in which the chest and abdomen were protected by a heavy, tough breast-plate, while the arms, legs and thighs were protected by plates joined by woven chains. The warrior also wore greaves and lightweight sandals. The overall outfit was laced and decorated with crests, gilt tassels and glittering insignia and base colours included black, crimson, gold, green, purple, silver, violet, and white.

The *samurai* sword was held with

LEFT: Samurai *in a variety of heroic poses as depicted by an unnamed 19th Century Western artist .*

FAR LEFT: A samurai *in a typically fearsome pose. Note the very elaborate crest on his helmet and the* sashimono – *the small banner on a pole attached to the warrior's back, which identified him in battle.*

T<small>YPICAL ARMOUR AND CLOTHING OF A</small> *SAMURAI* W<small>ARRIOR</small>

Kabuto = helmet (underneath is the *hachi-maki* (head cloth))
Maedate = crest
Nodowa = throat protector
Hoo-Ate = protective face-mask
Sode = shoulder plates
Wakibiki = armpit protectors
Kote = armour-protective sleeves
Donaka = body armour (cuirass)
Kusazuri = protective skirts
Yusake = leather gloves
Haitate = thigh guard
Fukigaeshi = folded back decorative addition to *Kabuto*
Sune-Ate = shin guards
Waraji = sandals
Tabi = socks
Skikoro = neck protector
Tehen = opening at crown of Kabuto
Mabi-sashi = peak (attached to *Kabuto* by rivets
Kia-Hon= leggings (usually linen)

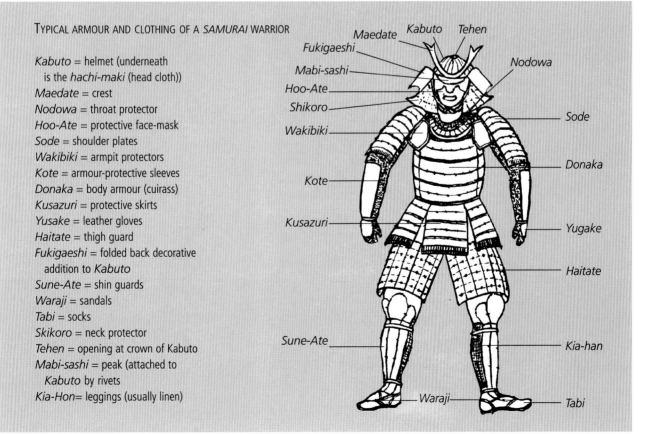

LEFT: A rare example of armour linked by *kawa-odoshi* (leather laces) rather than cords, which were criticised as becoming heavy and difficult to handle when wet.

ABOVE RIGHT: Suit of armour belonging to Toyotomi Hideyoshi (1536-1598), dating from 1568-1600. The large *mitsu kuwagate* (three-bladed crest) denotes a general of great importance.

BELOW: A leather-covered, wooden chest for storing and moving armour, with the crest of the Doi family (ca.1800).

LEFT: A suit of 18th Century armour, replete with very intricate and extensive lacing. Of particular note are the *hoate* (face mask), the large skirt to the *kabuto* (helmet) designed to protect the wearer's neck, and the leather *yugake* (gloves) with their prominent thumbs.

RIGHT: A fine suit of 18th Century armour (known as the *Daté* armor), with a *hotoke-do* (smooth surface cuirass). Note also the gauntlets, the very long skirt, *sune-ate* (shin guards) with the extension plates to protect the knee-cap, and the four cords wound around the waist, into which the two swords would be placed.

LEFT: A 19th Century suit of armor, made in the *haramaki* (belly-wrapping) style. Note that in this particular example the *kabuto* (helmet), and, in particular, the skirt, are extremely large, although the "fly-aways" and crest are of more modest proportions than in other examples.

RIGHT: An outfit completed in 1859 in the *oyoroi* (= great armor) style. Centuries of peace have resulted in an elaborate outfit, contrasting dramatically with the simplicity of that worn by Toyotomi Hideyoshi (above left, opposite). Note the elaborate *hoate* (face mask) with its exaggerated moustache and beard.

both hands, the main form of attack being a descending blow, so it was vital that the head and shoulders were well protected. The helmet was made of iron, lined with buckskin, with a flap made of articulated iron rings, which was attached at the sides and rear to protect the neck and shoulders. In addition, there were large, rectangular shoulder protectors, attached by cords, which were designed to absorb the force of a sideways stroke aimed at decapitating the victim. In battle a face-piece was also worn. It was made of lacquered iron, with removable mouth and

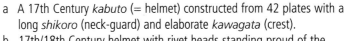

a A 17th Century *kabuto* (= helmet) constructed from 42 plates with a long *shikoro* (neck-guard) and elaborate *kawagata* (crest).
b 17th/18th Century helmet with rivet heads standing proud of the surface. Note that there is no *tehen* at the crown.
c 16th Century *kabuto* made from 62 plates, with a gold *tehen*. Below the helmet is an 18th Century *somen* (face mask).
d An elaborately decorated helmet bowl dating from the 16th/17th Century, constructed from seven rivetted plates.

nose pieces; it also frequently incorporated a large imitation moustache, which was intended to frighten the enemy.

Samurai were experts in fighting on horseback or on the ground, and practised both armed and unarmed combat. In the early part of the period the major emphasis was on fighting with the bow and arrow, with the swords being retained for close-in fighting and beheading enemies. However, experience of fighting the Mongols during their two 13th Century invasions, led to

e A Japanese helmet, but with very clear European influence on the design and shape; date unknown.

f Another European-style *kabuto* with a nape-guard of lacquered leather; mid-18th Century.

g A six-plate *kabuto* with stylized "flyaways'" and unusual crest, dating from the 19th Century, at the very end of the *samurai* period.

h Lacquered *mempo* (= face-guard) with an integral throat guard (early 19th Century). It was held in place by cords tied behind the head.

i Full face-guard with a large moustache. The wearer placed a *fukusa* (= cloth) over his chin before donning the mask.

a change in fighting style and *samurai* started to use their swords more and also to fight with spears and *naginata*. This move was accompanied by a further gradual change from fighting on horseback to foot combat.

Small hand-held shields were occasionally carried and archers sometimes stood behind a wheeled shield. Cavalrymen sometimes carried a large bolster-like stuffed bag, which not only provided protection against arrows but also enabled the arrows to be recovered and re-used. Shields were not, however, a normal part of the *samurai*'s outfit.

Samurai carried a number of distinguishing insignia. A personal symbol was carried on the front of the helmet, which in some cases was up to 3 feet (1m) high, and designs, which could be quite elaborate, included horns, fish, eagle and dragons. Most helmets also had a socket in the crown which could be used to house either a small distinguishing pennant or an ornament shaped like a pear. Finally, there was another socket at the top centre of the backplate, in which the clan banner was carried.

LEFT: A scene from the Genpei Seisui-ki, *the annals of the rise and fall of the Minamoto and Taira clans during the late 17th and early 18th Centuries by an un-named but contemporary artist.*

RIGHT: A somewhat satirical depiction of the domestic life of a samurai *in the Tokugawa period, when there was little real fighting to keep such warriors fully employed.*

BELOW RIGHT: The stirrup was an innovation imported from China and for many centuries they were of this platform type, rather than the arched type used in Europe. They were made of iron.

BELOW: Saddles were made of lacquered wood and the rope girth (not shown) passed under the horse's belly to be tied on top; it could be adjusted without the rider having to dismount.

こうとのち

ABOVE: Samurai *warriors were very skilled at using bows from horseback as this scene from the war between the Minamoto and the Taira clans shows.*

BOWS

Until the 16th Century, *yumiya* (= bows and arrows) were the most potent weapon used by warriors, the art of mounted archery being termed *bakyu-jutsu*. There were many styles, of which the *Ogasawara* was the best known, but, as later with the sword, *bakyu-jutsu* did not confine itself to the skills of mounted archery, but embraced matters of etiquette and decorum for *samurai*, as well.

Bows could be fired either by dismounted men, for example from a castle's defences, or from a horse, usually at the gallop, when the archer shot at right-angles to the direction in which the horse was moving. Bows were also the main weapons used in naval fights before ships came alongside each other and fighting became hand-to-hand. *Samurai* were required to carry out frequent archery practice, usually on horseback, and also to make arrows, many *daimyos* setting a daily quota.

The *yumi* (bow) was designed to be handled and used on horseback and thus could be neither too long nor too heavy. The bow had a deciduous wood base, usually of oak (*kashi*) and originally had a bamboo laminate on the forward (enemy's) edge, but a further bamboo laminate on the archer's side was added later. The very limited technology of the time meant that adhesives were of very poor quality, so the laminate was attached to the bow by a series of rattan bindings over most of its length, and the whole was lacquered to make it damp-proof. Many bows also had a handgrip, which was fitted at about one-third of the distance from the top of the bow to make it easier to use when on horse-back.

In earlier times the bow-string (*tsuru*) was fabricated from fibres obtained from the stems of two common plants: hemp (*cannabis sateva*) or ramie (*boehmeria nivea*). The resulting string was coated with wax, which not only gave it a hard, smooth surface but also provided a degree of damp-proofing. Later strings were made of silk impregnated with pine resin.

Fitting the string often required two men and was a process which could not be undertaken once combat had started. As a result, bows were strung before the battle and for

the more senior officers were carried in a frame by a bearer, ready for instant use.

Fighting arrows were made of bamboo, with three fletchings, made from bird feathers. Lengths varied, but were on average about 3 feet (1 metre) long. There were different types of arrow-head which were given descriptive names. One with a bulbous wooden head, which was perforated so that it emitted a whistling noise, was known as a "turnip-head," the noise being intended to alert the gods at the start of a battle to the deeds of valour which were about to be performed. The "frog's-crotch" was a U-shaped head with sharpened inside edges, intended to cut flags or sever helmetlacings. The "armour-piercer" was a plain bolt-head designed to penetrate a breastplate, while the purpose and effect of the "bowel-raker" needs little elaboration.

安德 天皇

Quivers (*ebira*) were made of leather, water-proofed paper or thin lacquered wood, and were often splendidly adorned. Unlike Western quivers, however, in which the arrows lay across the archer's back, the Japanese quiver made the arrows stand out towards the rear, making them easier to reach when on horseback.

Although the Japanese bow was inferior to modern composite bows in both penetration and accuracy, it was still a deadly weapon in skilled hands and until the musket arrived from Europe in the 17th Century it was the only weapon available in Japanese warfare for use at a distance. In their heyday, archers started a battle, frequently with duels between individuals, followed by a general exchange of fire, before a hand-to-hand engagement began.

ABOVE: News of defeat is brought to the Taira flagship at the Battle of Dan-no-Ura. Infant Emperor Antoku was grabbed by his grand-mother (in blue cowl) who leapt into the sea, drowning them both.

The performance of a bow depended upon the skill and strength of the archer, and *samurai* were, in general, more skilled than *ashigaru*. The extreme range of a bow was generally accepted to be about 3¹/₂ *cho* (415 yards/380 metres), although in battle the maximum effective range was more probably about 1 *cho* (120 yards/109 metres).

One of the most famous archers was Minamoto Tametomo (1139-1170) whose right arm was shorter than the left and who was reputed to be able to draw a bow which was too strong for the combined efforts of four ordinary men. His preferred missile was a shaft 5 feet (1.5 metres) long with an enormous bolt-head. At one point in his career, the tendons of his arms were cut and he was banished in a cage, although he managed to escape and fled to the island of Oshima, where he regained his strength. When a force was sent to recapture him he sank one of the approaching ships with armour-piercing arrows and then shut himself inside his house, set it alight and killed himself.

BELOW: A scene from the Gempei Wars. Note the hata jirushi, *the long standards attached to a crossbar, with those ashore identified by a two bar Rom (device) and those afloat by three bars (and which is repeated in the ships' superstructure).*

Another famous story about archery concerns the Battle of Yashima (1184), which was fought in shallow water. The Taira challenged the Minamoto to hit a fan suspended from a masthead, thus hoping to tempt them to waste their arrows, but Nasu-no-Yoichi, one of Minamoto-no-Yoshitsune's *samurai*, who was astride a horse, hit it at the first attempt.

SHAFTED WEAPONS

The *mochi-yari* (= spear) had replaced the bow as the mounted *samurai*'s principal weapon by the middle of the Civil War era. This was a simple weapon, based on a pole some 10-13 feet (3-4 metres) long, consisting of a hardwood centre, surrounded by bamboo laminations, which were bound in place by rattan thongs, and the whole lacquered to make it weatherproof. At the end of the pole was a straight iron blade, some 32 inches (80 centimetres) long. When used by mounted *samurai*, the *yari* was normally used as an impaling weapon, but

RIGHT: Naginata *were spears, usually about 16 feet (4.8m) long. There was a wide variety of heads, intended variously for stabbing, slashing, disembowelling, cutting a horse's tendons, and grabbing a man by his clothing.*

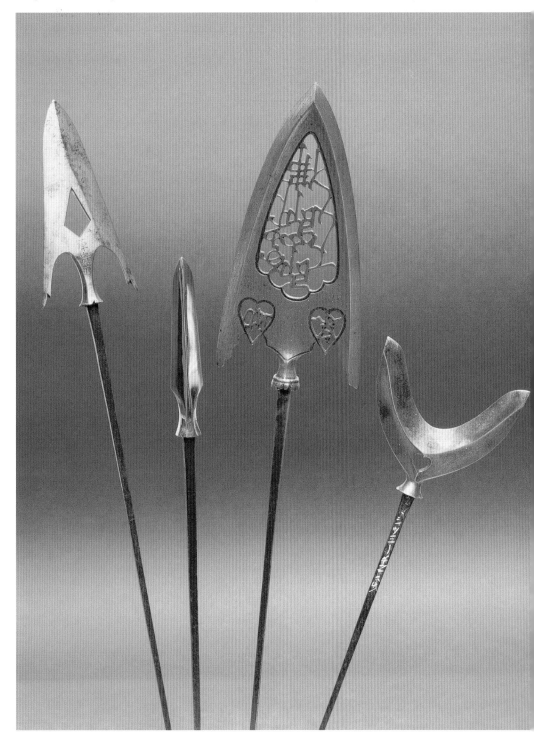

if it failed to penetrate the enemy's armour it could also be used to knock him to the ground, where he could be finished off with a sword.

In typical *samurai* fashion, many legends were told concerning illustrious spears, one of the most famous being *Nihongo*, which was originally owned by a *daimyo* named Fukushima Masanori (1561-1624), who was one of the "Seven Spears" who won great fame at the Battle of Shizugatake (1583). Shizugatake, a hill-top fortress, was being besieged by Hideyoshi, and Masanori used his spear in a fight with Haigo Gozaemon, on this occasion using it as a penetrating weapon to kill his opponent with a single thrust through the armpit. Unfortunately, Masanori later made a wager with another *samurai*, Mori Tahé, concerning the

amount of saké each could drink, and foolishly wagered *Nihongo* as the stake. When Tahé won he immediately claimed *Nihongo*, but the following day, the now sober Masanori asked Tahé to return the spear, which he refused to do and Masanori lost his beloved spear, a story perpetuated in a famous song, *Kurodabushi*.

` Later in the period pikes were adopted by the *ashigaru* (foot soldiers), which were known as *nagae-yari* or *naginata* (long-shafted spears). These were of varying lengths, the longest being about 16 feet (4.8 metres) long. These generally had a slightly curved blade and were used against horses to cut their tendons or disembowel them, or against the riders. *Naginata* were also used by warrior monks and occasionally also by *samurai* womenfolk.

There were also three shafted weapons designed to deal with aggressive people, but without killing them. The first of these was a form of grappling-iron with barbed tongues turned in every direction, resulting in a ball of hooks resembling an iron hedgehog, which was mounted on a 10 foot (3 metre) pole. This was designed to be thrust into the loose clothing, thus detaining a man whilst keeping him at bay but beyond sword reach. The second resembled a double-sided rake and was also mounted on a pole; this was intended to be thrust between a man's legs, bringing him down. The third such weapon was shaped like a large pitchfork, and was intended to pin an opponent to a wall or the ground, thus immobilizing him.

SWORDS

The sword has a very special place in Japanese history, having been produced for at least 2,500 years and with an authenticated history of approximately 2,000 years. Indeed, a sword is one of the three items which make up the sacred regalia, possession of which is the proof of the authenticity of the emperor. According to legend, this sword was found by the brother of Amaterasu, the Sun Goddess, in the tail of a dragon he had just slain. Recognising it as sacred, he promptly presented it to his sister, who named it *Ame-no-murakumo-no-hoken* (= sacred precious sword of the gathering clouds) and in turn presented it to the emperors of Japan.

During his reign, Emperor Sujin (10), a most religious man, decided to deposit the three sacred items in a purpose-built shrine, dedicated to the Sun-Goddess, in the village of Kasanui. Here they became the responsibility of a priestess, who had to be a virgin princess of the imperial blood. In about 4 AD the three sacred items were transferred to Uji in Isé province and in 110 AD one of Japan's great heroes, Prince Yamato-daké (d. 113 AD), passed through Isé on his way to conduct an expedition against the troublesome aboriginal tribe, the Ainu, in the north-eastern part of Honshu. When he stopped to worship at the shrine, the priestess took it upon herself to lend him *Murakomo*, keeping the prince's own sword as security.

During the subsequent campaign, the Ainu set fire to the underbrush, which threatened to engulf and destroy Yamato-daké and his entire army, but the prince was told by the Sun-Goddess to use the sacred sword and he was able not only to cut down the grass to stop it burning, but also to turn the flames back upon the Ainu, who promptly fled. In acknowledgement of this rescue, the prince renamed the sword *Kusanagi-no-tsurugi* (= grass-mowing sword) and returned it to Isé.

The main requirement for using the spear was muscular strength, but the sword required not only strength but a considerable degree of skill as well. As a result, *kenjutsu* (= the art of the sword) flourished. But, of even greater importance, *samurai* came to consider their swords to be the epitome of the "spirit of *bushido*," and the ultimate expression of the warrior's ethos.

The earliest type of sword was the *koto* (= old sword), which was made of cast bronze and

BELOW: Emperor Go-Toba and an assistant work on a sword blade, an activity regarded as a highly refined art-form. Swords were considered to possess mystical qualities and their manufacture had deep religious undertones.

continued in use until about the middle of the 6th Century AD when it began to be replaced by the *tsurugi*. This had a straight, double-edged blade, but was soon superseded at some time during the 8th Century by the modern curved, single-edged blade.

SWORDSMITH

The *katanakaji* (= swordsmith) was a highly respected member of society, whose place in Japan's carefully ordered social structure was at the top of the artisan and artist class. However, it was by no means unknown for *samurai* and noblemen to become involved in making swords, while at least one emperor, Go-Toba (82), practised the art. Swordsmiths and swordsmith schools attained a status in Japan somewhat similar to that of artists and their "schools" in the West and, like them, had instantly recognisable styles and periods. Thus, for example, many students of the art believe that Bizen province produced the finest swords, although, as with Western art experts, each school and *katanakaji* have their supporters. Some 12,000 swordsmiths have been identified by name and placing them in an order of merit is an impossible task.

Each sword was considered to possess its own mystical qualities and its fabrication was considerably more than a simple manufacturing process, being, instead, a highly refined art-form, with deep religious undertones. Thus, the *katanakaji* used a combination of iron, fire, water, wood and earth in its manufacture, with anvil, hammer, personal skill and spiritual guidance as the tools to forge the blade.

The design of the sword was tailored precisely to meet the needs of the *samurai* method of sword-fighting, which was quite different from that developed in the West and explains why there are such distinct differences between them. In the West, up to the late 16th Century swordsmen stood sideways on to each other in order to minimise the target they presented to the enemy, or faced each other with a shield in one hand and the sword in the other, and sought to defeat their opponents by a thrust with the point. Even when the shield was discarded and the sword was used for defence as well as for offence (by blocking and parrying) the intention was still to deliver the fatal blow by a thrust. As a result, the sword blade was straight, the handle short and a large guard was fitted to protect the hand, while the main design feature was the point; the edge of the sword was sharpened, but to nowhere near the standard of the Japanese sword. Early Japanese swords were based on a similar concept, and were copies of imported Chinese and Korean designs, with straight blades.

Japanese fighting developed in a different way, however, with swordsmen facing each other directly, holding the sword with both hands and using it both for attack and defence. Japanese swordsmen did not, therefore, carry a shield. Of even greater importance from a design point of view, they used the sword to cut and slash, as opposed to lunging. These requirements led to a blade that was long (to reach the opponent), had a sharp outer edge (to cut through the enemy) and was reasonably heavy (to give momentum to the swing). The blade was also required to be particularly stiff, but not brittle, so that it would withstand heavy blows and hard usage.

BELOW: Munechiica Inoru, a noted katanakaji *(sword-smith) working on a blade with the (very necessary) assistance of a spirit. Each blade required hundreds of hours of work before it could be passed to a* katanatogi *(sword sharpener).*

The *daisho* (sword) had a very special place in the *samurai's* life and there were two main types: the *daito katana*, also known as the *tachi* (= long sword), which was usually more than 24 inches (61cm) long, and the *koshigatana* (= short sword), which was between 12 and 24 inches (30-60cm) in length. By the start of the 17th Century, however, the *koshigatana* had evolved into two weapons, the *wakizashi*, the shorter of the two, and the longer *tanto*. Examples shown here are: long sword (*katana* or *tachi*) – a, b, c; d, e, g and short sword (*wakizashi* or *tanto*) - f, h, i, j, k.

a

b

c

d

e

f

g

h

i

j

k

The fabrication of a steel blade commenced with the *katanakaji* taking two pieces of different grades of steel and welding them together into a billet, which was then temporarily welded to a length of iron, which served as the handle for the remainder of the process. The steel billet was then heated to a red heat, folded back on itself with the two inner surfaces being welded to each other and then beaten out to its original length and cooled. This process was then repeated up to 20 times, following which the *katanakaji* beat the billet out into the planned size and shape.

Other blades were made with a relatively soft iron core surrounded by hard steel. The core and the surrounding material were beaten out and folded separately as described above, following which the hard steel was beaten into a V-shaped bar into which the iron billet was welded, the whole then being beaten out into the desired sword shape. The blade and tang were then finally shaped using a knife and file, and the *katanakaji* placed his signature (from about the 16th Century onwards) and other inscriptions (eg, date and place of manufacture) on the tang.

The next step was to temper the edge, which started with covering the blade with an even coating of a dampened mixture of iron-clay, river sand and charcoal powder, into which the *katanakaji* inscribed a line, parallel with and close

to the cutting edge. The coating between this line and the cutting edge was then removed, following which the blade was set aside until the remaining coating had dried. Using tongs to grip the tang, the *katanakaji* then heated the blade to the required temperature before plunging it into a vat of warm water for a predetermined time.

If the blade was then of a standard acceptable to the *katanakaji* he passed it to the *katanatogi* (= sword sharpener) who sharpened the edge and then polished the whole blade, a process which could take up to two months.

Finally, the sword-tester (again a highly esteemed profession) took the new blade and tested it. Until fairly recent times this was performed by cutting through the bodies of the dead or condemned criminals, and started with

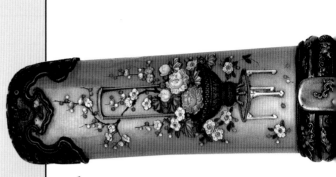

a

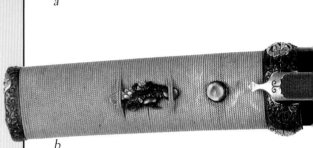

b

LEFT: Men face each other Japanese style using their swords to slash and cut; European style, opponents stood side-ways, using the sword to thrust and parry.

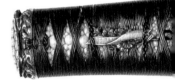

An assemblage of *tanto* (daggers) illustrating the high standard of workmanship lavished on such weapons. The top example (a) is a 19th Century weapon in the *Shibayama* style, completely covered in decoration. The next two are *Aikuchi tanto*: one handle (b) is completely covered by the *tsukaito* (= hilt thread), while in the other (c) the thread is wound in such a way as to leave gaps through which the *samé* can be seen. Below are two *tanto* made in about 1330 with the handle in the lower left (d) uncovered to show the *samé* (ray-fish skin) covering in all its glory.

c

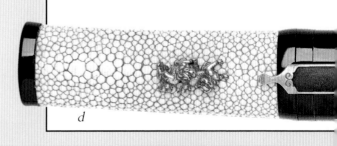

d

BELOW: Various pieces of sword furniture, the most prominent being the nine large *tsuba* (guard). The *tsuba* started as a round iron plate, intended to prevent an opponent's sword running along the blade and slicing into the swordsman's hand, but it became fashionable to decorate it with increasingly fanciful designs. Sometimes, as in the bottom left-hand corner, it was even made of fancy shapes.

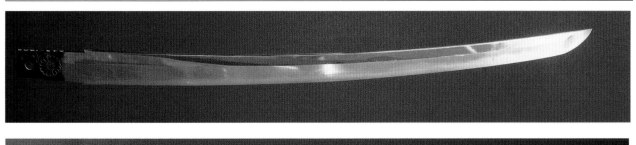

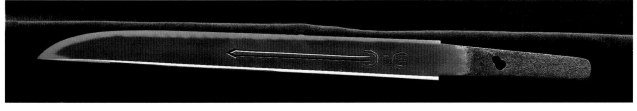

ABOVE TOP: Sword blade by katanakaji *Inoue Shinkai in 1673. Note the tang on the left with its proof marks and the hole for the bamboo or metal* mekugi *(retaining peg), which passed through to secure the hilt to the tang.*

ABOVE CENTRE: 19th Century sword blade by Umetada Myaju. Note the intricate and beautiful patterns worked into the cutting edge of the blade, making this as much a work of art as an instrument of war.

ABOVE BOTTOM: A tanto *(dagger) blade by Kagemitsu made in about 1330-1335. The* tanto *(also known as* shoto wakizashi*) was usually 12-24 inches (30-60cm) in length. Note the difference in finish between blade and tang.*

cutting through the small bones of the body and moving up to the larger ones. Latterly, the tests were performed on straw or bamboo bundles, which were assessed as having a resistance equivalent to that of a human body. The test results were usually recorded on the tang.

THE OTHER PARTS OF THE SWORD
The other parts of the sword were:

- *Tsuba* (= guard), a flat plate, usually circular, with a triangular hole at the centre, through which passed the tang. In war swords, the *tsuba* was made of metal, usually iron, steel, copper or brass, although particularly wealthy or influential warriors sometimes used gold. Some swords intended solely for ceremonial had *tsuba* made from leather, or wood with a leather covering. The *tsuba* was frequently highly decorated and some schools made them with holes.

- *Tsuka* (= hilt [handle]) was always made of wood, usually magnolia, with two halves glued together and covered with *samé*, the skin of a ray-fish. This, in turn, was usually covered by a *tsukaito* (= hilt thread), a silk-braid wrapping, which was wound in such a way as to form a series of lozenge-shaped holes, through which the *samé* could be seen. This wrapping combined its decorative effect with providing an extremely firm grip.

- *Mekugi* (= retaining peg), made of bamboo or metal and which passed through holes in the hilt and tang to hold the elements together.

- *Habaki* (= collar), which fitted over the upper end of the blade and the lower end of the tang.

- *Seppa* (= washers) were oval plates made of copper which fitted each side of the *tsuba*.

- *Fuchi* (= collar), which was fitted above the guard and acted as a retainer for the *tsukaito*.

- *Kashira* (= pommel-cap), which fitted over the end of the hilt.

- *Saya* (= scabbard) was made of magnolia in two halves and covered in a thick lacquer coating. The full-dress scabbard was normally a deep black colour, perhaps with a tinge of red or green.

THE CULT OF THE SWORD

A samurai wore two daisho (= swords), which he believed not only to be the "soul" of his warriorship, but also to represent the most sophisticated form of the beauty of killing. As a result, the sharper the sword, the more beautiful it was in the eyes of its owner and, as with bows and spears, he also gave them symbolic names. The *daito katana* (= long sword) was usually more than 24 inches (61 centimetres) long, while the *shoto wakizashi* (= short sword [dagger]) was between 12 and 24 inches (30-60 centimetres) in length.

The sword was accompanied by a most detailed etiquette. One *samurai* visiting another, for example, would leave his long sword with his servant, who then remained outside the house, or, if alone, the visitor would leave his sword in the vestibule, where one of the host's servants would pick it up using a silk napkin and place it on the sword-rack. At meetings where the participants did not know each other too well but had no reason to suspect each other, each man would withdraw his sheathed sword from his girdle and place it on the floor to his right; this indicated a degree of trust, since it would be difficult and time-consuming to draw the sword. If the circumstances were more suspicious, however, the sheathed sword would be placed on the owner's left, where it could be drawn more easily. In either case, the short sword was normally retained in the girdle, only being withdrawn on festal occasions or longer visits, when it would be withdrawn and placed by the servants on the house sword rack.

Challenges could be made in a variety of ways. First, if two *samurai* or *ronin* allowed their scabbards to clash, either accidentally or deliberately, this would be taken as a challenge to an instantaneous combat. This was akin to the Western concept of "throwing down the gauntlet" except that the fight took place on the spot, rather than at dawn the following morning. Ostentatiously twisting the sheath in the girdle was also tantamount to a challenge, while touching another's weapon in any way was considered to be a grave offence.

JITTE

The *jitte* (= mace) was an iron bar, some 24 inches (60 centimetres) in length. it was sometimes used in combat and was also used by *doshin* (= constable) during the Edo era. Some legends claim that *jitte* were used to break swords.

FIREARMS

The first firearm to enter Japan was a Chinese weapon, which was imported in about 1510, although it appears that it was examined with interest and then ignored. In 1542, however, a Chinese ship carrying three Portuguese passengers, the chief of whom was one Mendez Pinto, visited Tanegashima Island, bringing with them some European-manufactured arquebuses. Before departing, Pinto and his comrades had taught the Japanese how to manufacture both

ABOVE: The etiquette of the sword epitomised in 'The Challenge' in which two ronin *met and turned their backs on each other so that their scabbards clashed (*saya-até*), thus making a fight to the death inevitable.*

BELOW: The arrival of Europeans (in 1543) had its drawbacks, not least the introduction of firearms. At the Battle of Nagashino in 1575 Oda Nobunaga deployed no fewer than 3,000 men armed with matchlocks and totally defeated the enemy cavalry.

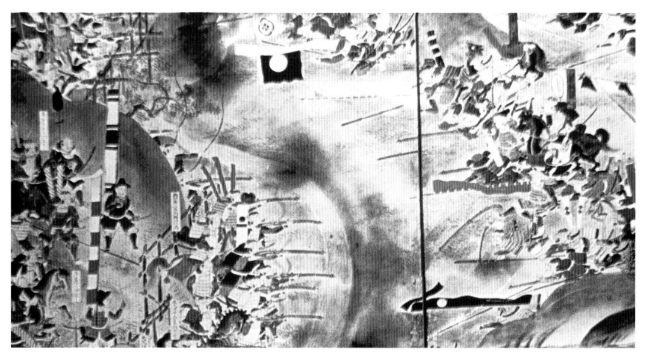

gunpowder and the arquebus, and soon every *daimyo* was competing to attract more Portuguese, but more importantly, their firearm technology, to his domain.

Within two years gunmaking had started in Japan, with the first weapons being produced in late 1544. One of the earliest to recognize the potential of these new weapons was Oda Nobunaga, and by 1553 he was able to parade five hundred *ashigaru* armed with them. He deployed these arquebusiers in what were, essentially, light infantry battalions, their first operational use being at the siege of Muraki Castle in 1554, when he used his arquebusiers to maintain a rolling volley. By the 1560s these weapons were in common use. However, due to the ban on European visitors (apart from a few Dutch on their island) the country's gunsmiths were isolated from further developments in Europe, in consequence of which the arquebus did not develop greatly.

The maximum range of the Japanese arquebus was about 330 yards (300 metres), although the maximum *effective* range was much shorter, probably about 66 yards (60 metres). Reloading time in ideal conditions was about 15-20 seconds, but probably somewhat longer in battle.

So far as can be discovered, no thought was ever given to developing a bayonet, which could be attached to the muzzle and used when at too close quarters for reloading to take place. In such a situation, the arquebusier had no alternative but to lay his weapon down and use a sword.

ABOVE: In a scene from a play, the samurai *on the right is holding a large pistol. Together with matchlocks, such weapons were available in large numbers but were never attributed with the same mystical qualities as swords, daggers and spears.*

NINJA WEAPONS

Their special role as infiltrators meant that the *ninja* had their own weapons requirements. Thus, the *ninja-to* (= *ninja* sword) was shorter than that used by the *samurai*, since the *ninja* required a weapon which could be wielded in a much more confined space. In addition, the scabbard of a *ninja-to* had a secondary function as a breathing-tube, enabling the user to conceal himself under water for long periods of time. Some *ninja-to* incorporated a second, much smaller, stabbing blade in the hand-grips.

Another *ninja* weapon was the *shuriken*, a term which encompassed a variety of small projectiles, which were designed to be hidden in the palm of the hand and then thrown at unarmed targets. One type was star-shaped and thrown with a spin, while another was needle-shaped and thrown like a dagger; many were tipped with poison.

The *kusari-gama* was a small crescent-shaped weapon, at the end of a long, thin chain, whose use required considerable skill, although in the hands of an expert it was a very dangerous weapon. The *ninja* held the end of the chain and swung it, so that the lethal end achieved considerable velocity and then projected it, the intention being either to seriously wound the enemy or to entangle his limbs or any weapon he might be holding. A variant, named either *manriki-gusari* or *fundo-gusari*, was identical in principle but had a weight at the end of the wire, rather than a cutting blade.

The *kunai* was a form of universal weapon/tool, consisting of a spearhead with a short handgrip, with an overall length of some 12 inches (30 centimetres). For fighting it could be used as a dagger, either for stabbing or throwing, while its more peaceful uses included knife, gimlet, shovel or hammer. When thrown its mass and design made it more effective and longer ranged than the *shuriken*, but, on the other hand, its size made it much more difficult to conceal.

Since their primary mission was obtaining information about the enemy, it followed that *ninja* had to escape to carry that information back to a commander who could use it. Thus, they needed to be good at escaping and to help them in this they used *makibishi*, which were small, multi-spiked objects, similar in concept to the European caltrop, which were designed so that one point would always point upwards. They were scattered by hand into the path of pursuers and were intended to penetrate their grass sandals and enter the soles of their feet, the points being frequently hooked to make removal more difficult. Towards the end of the era there was a more refined version, the *bakurai-bishi*, which exploded when stepped upon.

Chapter 5

SAMURAI WARS

Because the Japanese islands are separated from the Asian mainland the Japanese Empire tended to be relatively isolated from the wars and invasions that swept across Asia. The Japanese invaded Korea twice, in 203 AD and in 1592-98, but the only attempt at an invasion from outside came from the armies of Kublai Khan, in 1274 and 1281. Within the Empire, however, there was — at least until the beginning of the 17th Century — almost constant conflict. This included internecine warfare between the main clans, disputes between minor warlords, wars of imperial succession, conflict with the less developed tribes at the frontiers, especially the Ainu, and religious wars involving the various sects of warrior-monks and, later, Christians. This chapter highlights the more important conflicts, but it must be borne in mind that there were many more minor and localised conflicts going on, which formed a backdrop to these larger affairs.

Empress Jingu, the widow of Emperor Chuai, ordered the invasion of Korea in 203 AD and went with her troops even though she was pregnant. This painting by Sumiyoshi Hiroyuki (1755-1811), shows the empress aboard her flagship, escorted by ships carrying her army.

First Invasion of Korea

At their closest, Japan and the mainland of Asia are separated by the Straits of Tsu-shima, the Korean port of Pusan being 120 miles (193 kilometres) from the nearest point on the shore of the main island of Honshu. However, the Japanese have always controlled the island of Tsu-shima, which lies just off the most direct route and whose northernmost point is just 40 miles (64 kilometres) from Pusan. It is not known when the first contacts across this narrow stretch of sea began, but when Emperor Chuai (14) died in 200 AD while putting down a small rebellion, his successor and widow, Empress Jingu, conceived the idea of invading Korea. According to legend, she made the decision to proceed with the invasion whilst out fishing, by baiting a new hook with a grain of boiled rice, vowing that if she caught a fish she would take it as a sign of divine approval for the enterprise. Thus, when she successfully landed a fish, preparations were set in train and the fleet sailed in about 203 AD.

Jingu accompanied the army, even though she had discovered that she was pregnant. Once ashore, the Japanese exacted tribute from the stunned local tribes, few of whom had any idea

that there was a country over the eastern horizon, and then departed after a stay of about two months. On their safe return to Japan the expedition, in essence a naval raid, was considered a great triumph and referred to ever after as the first opportunity of making "the arms of Japan shine beyond the sea". Shortly after her return Jingu gave birth to a son, Ojin (15), and, somewhat unfairly, it was to him, rather than to his mother, that popular credit for this success was given.

Early Nine Years War (1051-1062)

Towards the end of the first millennium, signs of impending collapse increased and the 10th Century saw rebellions in the eastern provinces by Taira Masakado (d. 940), while a pirate, Fujiwara Sumitomo, established himself in the Inland Sea. These rebellions were both put down, although a long-running frontier war against the Emishi people in the north of Honshu

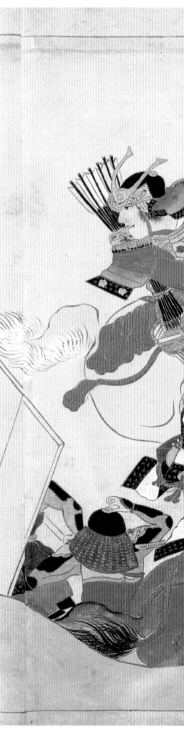

LEFT: *Minamoto Yoshiie (1041-1108), one of the great generals of the Heiean Dynasty, was so terrifying in battle that he earned himself the nickname,* Hachiman-taro. Taro *means "first-born son" while* Hachiman *was the Buddhist name for Ojin, the god of war.*

rumbled on.

In the Early Nine Years War the Abe clan, led by Abe Sadato, was brought back under imperial control by government forces led by Minamoto Yoriyoshi (995-1082), aided by his son, Minamoto Yoshiie (1041-1108). The main engagement was the Battle of Kawasaki (1057), where the Minamoto attacked a strong position in a raging blizzard and were repulsed. But they then conducted a fighting withdrawal in which Yoshiie, despite his youth, greatly distinguished himself. The war ended when Minamoto Yoshiie defeated Abe Sadato who was occupying the stockaded fortress of Kuriyagawa (1062). This campaign is of particular significance, in that it marks the first appearance of the group of professional warriors which came to be known as the *samurai*.

LATER THREE YEARS WAR (1086-1089)

Minamoto Yoshiie led the forces against the Kiyowara clan, led by Kiyowara Iehira. The major engagement in this war was the long drawn-out siege of Kanezawa (1086-1089) which ended in a fierce assault by Minamoto Yoshiie's forces.

HOGEN INCIDENT *(1155)*

In 1155 the Emperor Konoe (76) died suddenly at the age of 17 and the succession was not clear. The naming of Go-Shirikawa (77) caused serious disturbances, giving rise the following year to what became known as the *Hogen-no-Ran* (Hogen Incident) in which two rival groups of *samurai* fought each other in the streets of Kyoto during the course of one disastrous and bloody night. The Shirakawa-den palace was attacked by *samurai* led by Minamoto-no-Yoshitomo (1123-1160), who overcame their rivals led by Minamoto Tametomo (1139-1170). The engagement consisted mostly of arrow duels, but ended with the palace being set alight and destroyed.

HEIJI INCIDENT (1160)

This was followed in 1160 by the *Heiji-no-Ran* (Heiji Incident) in which Minamoto-no-Yoshitomo took advantage of the temporary absence of Taira-no-Kiyomori (1118-1181) from the capital to storm the Senjo palace. The attackers captured both Emperor Nijo (78) and his father, Go-Shirakawa (77) the "cloistered emperor", and murdered Michinori. On learning of these events, Kiyomori hastened back to the capital, and defeated the plotters in a violent counter-attack, only to discover that the emperor and his father had both escaped, the former disguised as a maidservant. Yoshitomo was subsequently murdered.

GEMPEI WARS (1180-1185)

A new conflict — the Gempei Wars — broke out in 1180, in which the Minamoto sought to overthrow the Taira. The opening engagement took place at Uji (1180), south-east of Kyoto, where the fighting monks of Nara heroically defended the bridge, but were driven back by the Taira, resulting in the suicide of Minamoto Yorimasa (1106-1180), a famous poet. Shortly afterwards (1180), the Minamoto forces again faced the Taira, this time at Ishibashiyama (= stone bridge mountain), but were again defeated. Their new leader, Minamoto Yoritomo (1147-1199), was forced to escape capture by hiding inside a hollow log. Undeterred, Yoritomo established another base at Kamakura, where he gradually built up his forces, and his first major confrontation came when the two armies found themselves facing each other from each bank of the Fujikawa river. The fast-flowing river proved an intractable obstacle, but the Taira, mistaking the noise of a large flock of wildfowl for a night attack, panicked and retreated.

There followed a succession of bloody and hard fought battles, with the tide gradually turning in favour of the Minamoto. Among the most significant engagements was the Battle of Kurikara (1183) in which Yoshinaka outgeneralled Taira Koremori (1129-1185). The Taira were traversing a mountain pass when they were fooled into thinking that they faced a greatly superior force and halted. Yoshinaka's main force then engaged the Taira in a long-range archery

ABOVE: The abduction of the former emperor, Go-Shirakawa, by Fujiwara-no-Nobuyori, in 1159. Possession of the person of a reigning or ex-emperor was frequently the crucial element in the struggles for power which frequently beset Japan during the era of the samurai.

ABOVE RIGHT: An incident during the Civil War in 1184. Minamoto Yoshitsune's army has arrived at the River Uji, but since the defenders have destroyed the bridge they are forced to ford the river on horseback, in which, despite hostile fire from Minamoto Yoshinaka's archers, they succeeded.

RIGHT: Another scene from the Battle of Uji River in 1184 as a lone samurai *plunges into the water, determined to be the first to reach and engage the enemy. .*

duel while other groups moved round into the Taira rear. The Taira were dealing with this new threat when darkness fell, whereupon Yoshinaka's main force released a herd of bullocks with flaming torches attached to their horns and the stampeding animals charged towards the Taira army, which withdrew in confusion and was heavily defeated.

The war did not go entirely the way of the Minamoto, however, and they were again defeated in a sea-battle at Mizushima and the land-battle of Muroyama (both in 1183). Minamoto Yukiiye (d. 1186) and Minamoto Yoshinaka (1154-1184), Yoritomo's uncle and cousin, respectively, took the Imperial capital at Kyoto in 1184. The infant Emperor Antoku (81) having been carried away, Go-Toba (82) was proclaimed emperor in his place. Yoshinaka and his Minamoto troops were so ruthless, however, that Go-Shirikawa (77) incited the warrior-monks of the Hiyeizan and Miidera monasteries to join in a campaign against the interlopers.

新中納言平知盛

相模五郎

ABOVE: The Battle of Dan-no-Ura in May 1185, between the Taira, with 500 junks and the Minamoto with 700. The Taira were defeated and many committed suicide, but the Minamoto then hunted down and killed every other male member of the defeated clan they could find.

Yoshinaka managed to overcome them in a new outbreak of fighting which ended with the successful siege of the Hojujiden palace, following which the two abbots were beheaded and Go-Shirikawa was imprisoned.

The Minamoto, led by Minamoto Yoritomo, defeated the Taira at the Battle of Yashima (1184) but most of the Taira escaped. The war culminated in the Battle of Dan-no-Ura (1185), a naval battle in which the Taira were decisively defeated; losses during the fighting were severe, but then most of those who survived committed suicide.

FIRST MONGOL INVASION (1274)
Once he had overthrown the Sung dynasty in China, Kublai Khan cast around for new

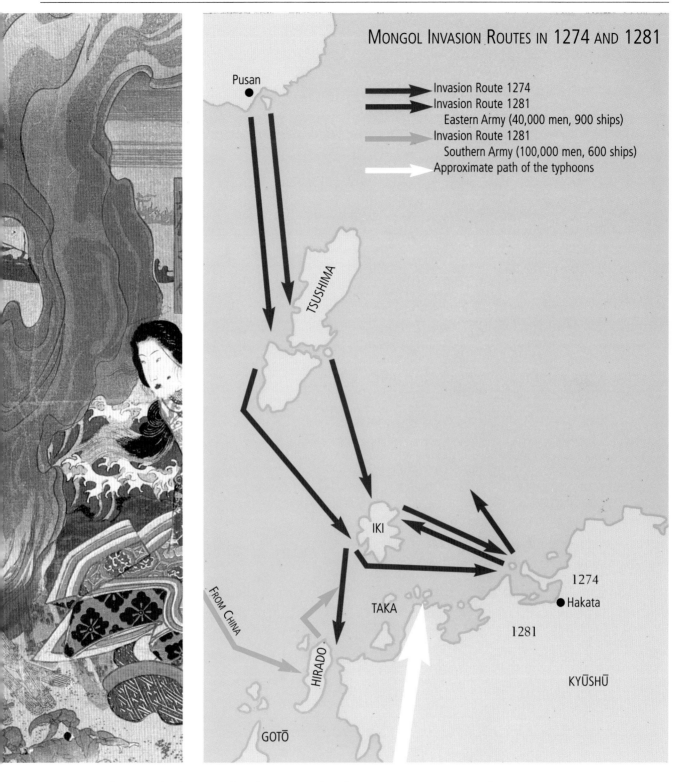

MONGOL INVASION ROUTES IN 1274 AND 1281

Invasion Route 1274

Invasion Route 1281
Eastern Army (40,000 men, 900 ships)

Invasion Route 1281
Southern Army (100,000 men, 600 ships)

Approximate path of the typhoons

Pusan

TSUSHIMA

IKI

FROM CHINA

TAKA

HIRADO

GOTŌ

1274

●Hakata

1281

KYŪSHŪ

countries to bring under his control and sent several embassies to Japan, requiring that country to acknowledge his suzerainty. Six such embassies were peremptorily rejected by the *shikken* (= regent), Hojo Tokimune (1251-1284), as a result of which an infuriated Kublai Khan despatched a punitive expedition, consisting of some 10,000 men embarked in Korean ships. The force started its operations by capturing the islands of Tsushima and Iki to serve as forward bases and then conducted its main landing at Hakata Bay (Aajkozaki) in northern Kyushu. A hastily assembled Japanese army attacked the invaders near the beaches, but despite a numerical superiority the Japanese were repulsed. Part of the invasion fleet was then wrecked in a storm and since more Japanese reinforcements were arriving every day, the Mongols reembarked in the remaining ships and returned to Korea.

SECOND MONGOL INVASION (1281)

The Japanese continued to refuse to accept Kublai Khan's authority and when a further embassy arrived in Japan all nine members of the group were beheaded. In 1279 the Japanese were in the middle of assembling a force to repel the invasion which they realised must come when yet another embassy arrived and, once again, all its members were beheaded.

This time Kublai Khan sent a much larger force, with one army sailing from north China and a second from Korea, the total probably coming to some 50,000 men. Again the Mongols occupied both Tsushima and Iki, and then sailed for the mainland, where a large Japanese army was awaiting them, and a series of violent sea and land clashes then followed. At sea the Japanese carried out a series of raids against the Chinese ships, with varying degrees of success, but despite this the Chinese force managed to establish itself ashore. The Chinese were, however,

ABOVE: *The Onin War, in essence a dispute over the succession of the* shogun, *took place in and around Kyoto over a period of eleven years. The* shogun *himself (Yoshimasa) was a helpless bystander, the two leaders died of sickness and the war ended with no clear-cut victory.*

LEFT: *When the Mongols attempted to invade Japan their fleets were hit by violent storms, spreading the belief that Japan was protected by gods.*

ABOVE LEFT: *During the second Mongol invasion one army got ashore, but a typhoon hit their fleet, sinking many ships; the remainder escaping to Korea. The Chinese troops ashore were then rounded up and killed.*

unable to advance more than a few miles inland, while the Japanese were unable to drive them into the sea. In desperation the Japanese petitioned the gods to come to their aid and shortly afterwards a typhoon struck the Chinese fleet, causing a great amount of damage and sinking a large number of junks. The surviving ships were blown far out to sea and then made for Korea, while the troops ashore, cut-off and without any supplies, were finished off by the exultant Japanese. Kublai Khan promised to make another invasion but it never happened, while the Japanese attributed their salvation to the god Isé and the sacred wind, which was named *kamikaze*, a name which was to reappear much later in Japanese history, with dire consequences.

CIVIL WAR (1331-1333)

The Emperor Go Daigo (96) led a revolt against Hojo rule, assisted by *samurais*, Kitabatake Chikafusa and Kusonoki Masashige (1294-1336). In the initial round, Go-Daigo was defeated and captured, but managed to escape to continue the revolt and eventually succeeded when several Hojo generals, including Ashikaga Takauji (1305-1358), deserted to his side, enabling him to capture the Hojo stronghold at Kamakura. When Go-Daigo refused to appoint him *shogun*, Takauji revolted in 1335.

WARS BETWEEN THE COURTS (1333-1392)

Japan was ravaged by a bitter civil war for 56 years as Go-Daigo and his successors fought the Ashikaga *shoguns* and their puppet emperors. Finally, in 1392, an Ashikaga envoy persuaded the true emperor at Yoshino, Go-Kameyama (99), to abdicate and relinquish the sacred imperial regalia, thus enabling the Ashikaga *shoguns* to claim their emperor as the rightful ruler and to establish their own control over all Japan. By this time, however, the *daimyo* had established themselves in all parts of the country and the Ashikaga *shoguns* never managed to impose their control over these hereditary, feudal lords, who attacked their neighbours and seized land.

WAR OF THE MONKS *(1465)*

This was a conflict between the warrior-monks of Enryakui and of Honganji. The latter were defeated and their monastery was completely destroyed.

ONIN WAR *(1467-1477)*

The Onin War was nominally a war of succession within the Ashikaga family, but in reality it was a power struggle between two great warlords: Yamana Mochitoyo (1404-1473) and his son-in-law Hosokawa Katsumoto (1430-1473). Both died during the war (1473) but the struggle continued among their followers and in the provinces until the early 1490s.

RENEWED CIVIL WAR *(1493).*

Hosakawa Masamoto (1466-1507), the son of Hosokawa Katsumoto, led a revolt to drive the *shogun* Yoshitame (1465-1522) from Kyoto. Masamoto then set up a puppet *shogun*, the 16-year-old Ashikaga Yoshizumi (1478-1511), although the latter ruled only briefly, being deposed when Yoshitane's forces returned. Meanwhile, Hosakawa Masamato continued his intrigues and was eventually murdered.

BELOW: Samurai *warriors had to keep their fighting skills at their peak, especially during the period known as the "Epoch of the Warring Country", when local wars among feudal lords had become endemic.*

RIGHT: Shogun *Yoshimitsu (1358-1408) was a cultured man who built a villa, which included the Golden Pavilion, seen here. The name derived from the gold-leaf covering the outer walls of the central and upper floors. The building was almost destroyed by fire in 1950 but has been restored.*

EPOCH OF THE WARRING COUNTRY (1467-1568)

By the 16th Century local wars among feudal lords had become endemic and the period is still remembered in Japanese history as the "Epoch of the Warring Country". This started with the Onin War in 1467 and continued until 1568, by which time the authority and prestige of both the emperor and the *shogun* decreased markedly.

OVERTHROW OF BUDDHIST MONASTERIES (1571-1580)

One of Nobunaga's particular aims was to bring the overpowerful monasteries to heel and he did so systematically and with utter ruthlessness. Many monasteries were huge, with stone walls and moats, while the so-called "warrior-monks" maintained large stocks of armour and weapons, to be used either by themselves or by armies in their pay. These monasteries not only intervened in the wars of others (sometimes even supporting both sides to ensure that the winner was in their debt) but also engaged in conflicts with each other.

The largest of these monasteries, and the one which Nobunaga selected as the start-point for his campaign, was at Hiei, which had been a sacred site for over a thousand years and whose grounds included no fewer than 500 temples, shrines and houses, providing accommodation for many thousands of monks. The attack took place on September 29/30 1571 and the inhabitants of the town at the foot of the mountain moved up to the monastery, seeking protection and leaving their abandoned town to be burnt to the ground by Nobunaga's forces. Nobunaga then encircled the mountain and his men gradually ascended, killing anybody — man, woman or child — they found. By the end of the second day some 20,000 people had been killed and the various monasteries and shrines completely obliterated.

Next was another fortified temple at Osaka, owned by the Shin sect of Buddhists, who were one of the principal opponents of Nobunaga and who had committed the fatal error of providing shelter to some rebels who had ambushed and killed several of his generals. The castle consisted of five interconnected fortresses surrounded by high walls and was occupied by several thousand priests and warriors, as well as many women and children. Nobunaga's men surrounded this complex and one of the first actions came when several thousand people attempted to slip through the cordon of besiegers on a particularly dark night. They were detected and slaughtered and a junk containing their ears and noses was floated down to the castle, a grim foretaste of the fate that might well await the remainder of the garrison.

Below~: The Battle of Shizugatake Pass (1583). Hideyoshi, with 20,000 cavalry, made a 50 mile (80km) forced march in one day to attack a force under Sakuma Morimasa. Hideyoshi's attack, shown here, was led by a group immortalised as the "Seven Spears of Shizugate".

The siege was long drawn out and involved huge casualties on both sides but, when the besiegers had taken three of the fortresses and the remaining defenders were penned up in the remaining two, the emperor intervened by sending a delegation which persuaded the abbot to surrender; the castle was taken over by the government, the priests were dispersed to other monasteries, and the other surviving occupants were pardoned.

INVASION OF KOREA (1592-1598)

Hideyoshi intended to invade China by way of Korea, but the Koreans refused to allow the Japanese forces unimpeded passage. As a result, the Japanese had to fight all the way, starting with the port of entry, Pusan, which was taken on April 13 1592. The Japanese then struck north, taking the fortress of Tongnae (April 15), brushing aside a Korean force at Sangju (April 24), and defeating a major Korean army at Ch'ungju (April 27). A few days later the Japanese army entered the deserted capital, Seoul, but after the briefest of pauses they pressed on northwards, reaching the Imjin River in mid-May and taking Pyong-Yang on June 16 1592. This was an astonishing advance, traversing the entire length of the country, with several major engagements fought on the way, and which had lasted just 64 days.

Meanwhile, another Japanese force had been pushing up the east coast and by mid-July was as far north as Haejonch'ang, where a battle took place around a grain warehouse, whose contents were needed to supply the Japanese troops. The Japanese, under Kato Kiyomasa (1562-1611), one of the most famous of the *samurai*, prevailed, luring the Koreans into a swamp, where they were massacred.

All was not well at sea, however, and at the Battle of the Yellow Sea (July 1592) a Korean fleet under Admiral Sin Yi Sung intercepted and attacked a Japanese reinforcement convoy. The Koreans were completely successful, with at least 59 Japanese ships being sunk and the convoy destroyed.

One of the consequences of the Japanese impetuous rush to the north was that they had failed to quell those Korean forces which were not on either of the two routes. Thus, in October they had to send a force to lay siege to a Korean garrison in Chinju Castle, but when their troops encircling the castle were threatened from the rear by guerrillas they were forced to withdraw.

Meanwhile, the Koreans had

Haejŏngch'ang ●
1592 ✕

THE JAPANESE CAMPAIGN IN KOREA: 1592-1598

● P'YONG-YANG
✕ 1592-93

✕ 1592 Imjin River
Yonan ●
1593 ✕ ● Byŏkchekwan
Haengju ● ● SEOUL
1593 ✕

● Ch'ungju
✕1592
● Ch'ongju
Sanju ● ✕1592

Kyŏngju 1593 ●
Kumsan 1592   Ulsan ●
●   1597-98 ✕
Chonju 1592   Chinju 1592, 1593   ● Tongnae 1592
●   ✕✕
Namwon 1597   Kinhae Mason ● ● PUSAN ✕ 1592
● ✕ Sunch'ŏn ●
Myongyang   Sach'ŏn ●
            1598 ✕
            Area of ten
            separate naval
            engagements   TSUSHIMA
            in 1598

called upon the Chinese for military aid. The first Chinese troops attacked the Japanese garrison in Pyong-Yang in late 1592, only to be defeated by a trick. But they regrouped and returned in February 1593 and the Japanese, finding themselves greatly outnumbered, withdrew southwards towards Seoul. The Japanese made a stand at Byockchekwan, just north of Seoul, with their forces in three groups, two on the forward slope of the hill and the third to

ABOVE: An incident during the military career of Toyotomi Hideyoshi (1536-1598), when his ship was stranded in the treacherous Kanmon Channel, the narrow gap which separates the islands of Kyushu and Honshu. Born of humble parents Hideyoshi eventually ruled all of Japan.

the rear. The Chinese pushed the Japanese back but, when the Chinese army accidentally became split into two, the Japanese seized the advantage and both sides became locked in close combat, from which the Japanese emerged victorious.

By now, however, the huge numbers of the Chinese forces were beginning to tell and the Japanese were slowly driven back towards the port of Pusan, although the Japanese did score one success when they laid siege to the castle at Chinju for the second time. On this occasion, after a hard-fought battle, they succeeded, but by 1594 the Japanese were pinned down in a pocket around Pusan and the Chinese withdrew, leaving their allies to conduct the peace negotiations.

These negotiations, however, proved to be very protracted and inconclusive and in 1597 Hideyoshi despatched reinforcements, which enabled the Japanese to break out in 1597, once again threatening Korea and bringing China back into the war. The Japanese forces took the castle of Namwon (August 13 1597), while a 5,000-strong Japanese garrison at Ulsan successfully withstood a siege by a Chinese/Korean army of some 80,000 men.

At the Battle of Chinhae Bay (November 1598) the Korean Admiral Sin Yi Sung attacked the Japanese fleet and won a second great victory. He was killed, but some 200 Japanese ships were sunk and the remainder fled to Kyushu. With their supply line effectively severed and the news that Hideyoshi had died in Japan, the remaining invaders had little choice but to make peace and return home.

WAR OF SUCCESSION (1598-1600)

When Hideyoshi died in 1598 there was a brief war of succession, in which the main

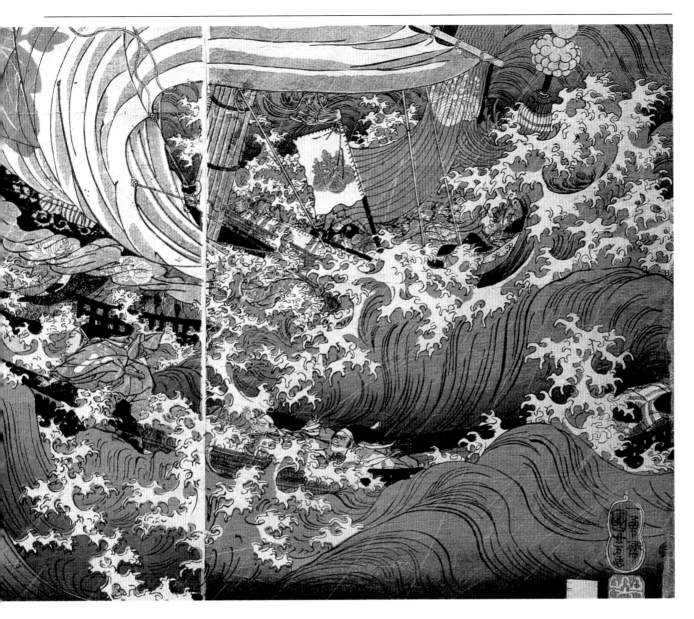

engagement was the Battle of Sekigahara (October 21 1600) in which Ieyasu (74,000 troops) totally defeated a coalition force (82,000 troops).

Siege of Osaka Castle (December 1614- June 1615)

After Sekigahara, Hideyoshi's son, Hideyori, retired to Osaka Castle, where increasing numbers of *ronin* gathered. The Edo forces under Ieyasu then besieged the castle in December 1614 but a truce was agreed in January 1615. The besieging forces took advantage of the cessation of hostilities to fill in the outer moats and in June they stormed and captured the fortress.

Shimabara Revolt (1637-38)

Despite the firm control exercised by the Tokugawa *shogunate*, there were occasional upheavals, one of the largest of which occurred in 1637. This was the result of increasing cruelty by Matsukura Shigeharu (d. 1638), a much-hated *daimyo*, who ruled the Shimabara peninsula. One of his favourite pastimes was the "straw raincoat" which was forced on an unfortunate peasant and then set alight. Japanese peasants had become used to a degree of cruelty, but Matsukura became so extreme in his methods that his people, most of whom were Christian, rebelled. The rebels took over a dilapidated castle at Hara, which they hastily refurbished, and then courageously resisted a long siege, forcing the *daimyo* to send for help from the *shogun*. The *shogun's* troops arrived the following year and eventually took the castle, following which they annihilated the rebels and their families, not even the children being spared.

Chapter 6

THE END OF THE SAMURAI

The Tokugawa *shogunate* saw an unprecedented two-and-a-half centuries of relative domestic peace, during which the position of the *samurai* was secure. They were the only group allowed to wear swords, a very visible sign of their status. By statute, their status was hereditary and they enjoyed a lifetime income from the state. Despite this, they were warriors without a conflict and their income remained constant and did not even keep pace with inflation. This enforced and prolonged period of inactivity led them to seek new ways to justify their existence. The more intellectual among them searched in history for heroes upon which to model themselves and for a philosophy which would help them to codify their conduct. This led to the romanticised image of historical figures in *samurai* history and to the intensification of the *bushido* code.

This period ended in the middle of the 19th Century, with the arrival of the United States Navy squadron, led by Commodore Matthew Perry. That event, albeit momentous, was not the cause of the change, but rather the catalyst that accelerated a process that was already well under way.

The *sakoku* (= closed country) policy had been implemented since the repression of the Christians in the 17th Century. Under this, no Japanese was allowed to travel abroad and foreign access was restricted to two ports: Nagasaki, which could be used by small Chinese vessels, and the tiny island of Deshima, where a Dutch trading post was permitted to operate.

The first, and somewhat tentative acknowledgement of the outside world came in 1720, when the *shogun* Tokugawa Yoshimuné lifted the ban on European books and study, following which a few personal visits were also made, but foreign pressure on Japan was steadily increasing. The Russians, who had been extending their territories eastwards for several centuries, were rebuffed twice, first in 1792 and again in 1804, following which they attacked several Japanese settlements in the Kurile Islands as a reprisal. Also in the early 1800s, a British frigate, claiming to be in need of supplies and initially turned away, sent a party ashore at Nagasaki to take hostages, who were later exchanged for supplies. In 1813-14 some British ships tried to trade at Nagasaki, using the Dutch flag as a subterfuge, but again without success. Then, from the 1820s onwards, American whalers started operations off the Japanese coast, their steamships killing whales in full view of Japanese watchers; some even entered harbour, although they received a hostile reception, and a number of shipwrecked whalers were believed to be held in prison.

Such random and small-scale attempts to enter were not a significant threat to Japan, but news of the First Opium War (1840-1842) between China and Great Britain caused considerable alarm. This war arose from the Chinese refusal to allow British merchants to bring opium into their country through the port of Canton. Following verbal disputes, the Chinese carried out reprisals against the European community (November 1839) resulting in a British punitive expedition which operated along the Chinese coast, eventually forcing the Chinese to sign the Treaty of Nanking (August 29 1842), under which they were forced to cede Hong Kong, to open five "treaty ports" and to pay an indemnity of US$20million. To the *shogunate*, the possibility of the same type of unequal treaty being imposed on Japan was clear, but their

ABOVE: The last Tokugawa shogun, Keiki, was appointed in October 1866, but proved to be indecisive. His army was decisively beaten in 1868 by imperial forces and he took shelter aboard an American vessel. Refusing to commit seppuku, he resigned, retiring to live as a private gentleman.

RIGHT: A satirist depicts "Samurai in Times of Peace" showing them eating, drinking, playing games and dreaming of glory in times gone by, while the suit of armour and muskets lie unused. Such was the fate of the samurai *during the long peace of the Tokugawa shogunate.*

RIGHT: *Commodore Perry (1794-1858) delivered a letter in 1853 asking the* shogunate *to end its "closed door" policy. This painting shows his seven warships entering Edo Bay in January 1854 to receive the reply. But the* shogunate *had no option and gave in, ending centuries of isolation.*

only response was to become even more determined to retain the "closed country" policy.

However, there were internal factors involved as well. The threat of foreign expansion in Asia happened to coincide with an increasing feeling of discontent among various elements of Japanese society. Some resented the power exercised by the self-satisfied and highly conservative *shogunate*, while the more scientifically minded argued that Japan needed to make use of European technology and science if it was to gain its rightful place as a great nation on a global scale.

An additional problem was that several of the early Tokugawa policies were now exercising an unexpected long-term effect quite opposite to what had originally been intended. In the early years of their power the Tokugawas had given their allies fiefdoms around the capital to ensure their safety. They had also ordained that all *daimyos* should maintain residences in Edo, in which they had to spend at least half of each year, and where they were required to leave

members of their families when they visited their domains. The first consequence of this was that the domains closer to Edo became richer and the second that the time taken in travelling and its cost increased proportionately with the distance from the capital, both of which increased the outlying *daimyos'* resentment. This brought in the third factor, which was that the farther the *daimyos'* fiefdoms were from the capital, the more difficult it was for the *shogunate* to supervise them.

As a result, by the 1840s many of the outlying provinces were seriously disaffected, none more so than Choshu and Satsuma in the south-west, whose long coastline was much more vulnerable to foreigners seeking to penetrate into the forbidden empire. The *daimyos* of both provinces were aware of much of what Europe and the United States had to offer, especially where military hardware was concerned. The *daimyo* of Satsuma established arsenals and mills, and also started the teaching of Dutch and English languages, turning his capital at

Kagoshima into a centre of industry and education.

The *shogunate* showed astonishing complacency in the face of this gradually increasing discontent, but on July 7 1853 there came a totally unexpected development, when the US Navy's Commodore Matthew Perry and his squadron of seven steamships sailed into Edo Bay. Perry was adamant that a treaty should be concluded, although he was under the mistaken impression that he was negotiating with a representative of the emperor when, in fact, he was dealing with the *shogunate*. The Treaty of Kanegawa was eventually signed on March 31 1854, although, for the Japanese, the early results of opening the country to foreign trade were not impressive. There was rampant price inflation and foreign diseases entered the country, accompanied, as so often happens in times of calamity in Japan, by an unusual number of earthquakes, typhoons, floods, fires and storms.

RIGHT: The signing of the treaty with the Americans opened a bitter internal quarrel. Here the chief minister, Ii Nawosuke, who had signed the treaty, is attacked outside the Sakurada Gate of Edo Castle. Despite an escort of fifty men, the 17 samurai *attackers were able to kill Ii.*

In the middle of all this upheaval, the *shogun*, Tokugawa Iemochi, died in 1859, but the process of finding a successor was badly mishandled by the senior official, the regent, Ii Nawosuke, who made a singularly ill-judged choice: the 12- year-old Prince of Kii. Those who expressed opposition were imprisoned, exiled, or, in some cases, beheaded, and matters were made even worse when it became known that Ii had ratified the treaty with Perry without consulting the emperor. This resulted in many Japanese patriots swearing revenge for such an insult and Ii was assassinated on March 23 1859, following which the patriots' rage turned on the foreigners, many of whom were murdered in the streets.

The first acts of the new government accelerated the rate of change. First, it revived the ancient custom of the *shogun* travelling to Kyoto to pay homage to the emperor, although since it was some 250 years since this highly symbolic act had last taken place many people had

ABOVE: *Early contacts with the outside world proved painful and there were several major "incidents". Here a combined operation by British, Dutch, French and US warships on September 6 1863 against the Choshu clan culminates in a landing by US Marines to destroy guns at Shimonoseki*

RIGHT: *An authentic, but nameless, samurai, photographed in 1865, wearing the traditional clothes of the warrior class. His status is identified by his unique hairstyle and his two swords, the longer (*daito katana*) held firmly in his left hand, the shorter (*shoto wakizashi*) tucked into his belt.*

forgotten that it existed. Next, the newly appointed prime minister, Matsudaira Yoshinaga, *daimyo* of Echizen, abolished the rule that *daimyos* had to reside in Edo and as soon as they knew of this all *daimyos* then present in the city departed. The vast majority of the aristocracy now paid ostentatious respects to the emperor's court, while the *shogunate* attempted to restore its prestige by seeking to close the ports and persuade the foreigners to leave.

By now the country was polarising between the supporters of the emperor and those of the *shogunate*, and there was considerable turmoil. Thus, when the emperor issued an order that the foreigners were to be expelled, the Choshu clan erected some coastal artillery batteries. To add to the confusion, the *shogunate*, which was seeking to persuade foreigners to depart, but in an orderly fashion, belatedly realised that, under the treaty it had itself negotiated, it was responsible for foreigners' safety. As a consequence, the *shogunate* ordered the guns to be dismounted, which the Choshu clan refused to do.

THE KAGOSHIMA AND SHIMONOSEKI AFFAIRS

This explosive situation was then compounded by two separate incidents involving foreigners. The first, the "Richardson Affair", took place on September 14 1862 at Kagoshima, when a large Japanese procession was proceeding along the *Tokaido* highway. The Japanese provincial authorities had issued a polite notice to the foreign community requesting them to avoid the highway during the time that the procession was due to pass, since interference with its progress was such a serious matter that even a Japanese crossing its path would be put to death on the spot, and the authorities wished to avoid any incident involving foreigners.

Unfortunately, this advice was ignored by a group of British people – three men and a woman, all unarmed – out for a ride (it was a Sunday), who not only went on the road, but at the behest of one of the group, a Mr Richardson, deliberately tried to ride through the procession. The retainers in the procession took this as a gross affront, promptly attacking the interlopers, killing Richardson and wounding the other two men, but leaving the woman untouched.

The British immediately issued a demand for reprisals and compensation, which the Japanese initially refused, and seven British warships duly arrived off Kagoshima on August 11

1863. Even though negotiations were still under way, the crews of the British ships suddenly seized three Japanese steamships lying in the roadstead, and then bombarded the city and its fortresses for two days, causing extensive damage, sinking five junks, flattening many buildings and taking several lives. This left the Japanese with no option but to pay the indemnities: £100,000 from the central government and £25,000 by the Satsuma clan (£5million and £1.25million, respectively, at current prices).

Meanwhile, the Choshu clan had become involved in a series of anti-foreigner incidents at Shimonoseki. The first of these took place on June 25 1863 when an American vessel, SS *Pembroke*, on its way from Yokohama to Shanghai, was warned off by a blank round fired from a nearby fort as it was about to drop anchor off the port of Shimonoseki. The captain refused to move and his ship was attacked the following day by two small warships belonging to the Choshu clan, but escaped undamaged.

On July 11 1863 the same forts fired blank warning shots at two other European warships, the French *Kien Chang* and the Dutch *Medusa*. When this had no effect they fired live rounds, causing some casualties and damage, whereupon the French put a party of marines ashore who destroyed one of the batteries.

In response to the *Pembroke* incident, the US minister despatched a gunboat, USS *Wyoming*, which arrived off Shimonoseki on July 16 1863 and, having been attacked by two Japanese warships supported by six shore batteries, the Americans proceeded to shell their assailants. Eventually, having meted out much retribution, but having in its turn suffered five killed, six wounded and much damage, the *Wyoming* returned to Yokahama.

The Western powers now decided that much more effective retribution was needed and assembled a fleet of 17 warships (British - 9; French - 3; Dutch - 4; US - 1), together with a battalion of US Marines, the British taking part despite having suffered no loss themselves. This fleet bombarded the Shimonoseki forts on September 5-6 1863, at the end of which the marines went ashore, took the batteries and destroyed the guns. Following this the four foreign powers demanded and received US$3million compensation, which was paid between 1865 and 1875.

CIVIL WAR

Faced by the first military challenge for two-and-a-half centuries, the *samurai* had proved ineffective, since they had neither the technology nor the training to do more than offer token challenges to the Europeans and Americans. Their way of waging war could not counter the foreigners' machineguns and long-range artillery, but there was to be one final outbreak of warfare and fighting using the traditional armies and traditional methods.

The first response of the Choshu clan to these setbacks against the foreigners was to step up the resistance to them and in September 1863 they suggested that the emperor should make an imperial progress to Yamato, as a signal that he would take the field in person against the hated foreigners. This was initially hailed as a sound suggestion and arrangements had already been put in hand when suspicions arose that the Choshu plan was merely a cover and that they intended to kidnap the emperor. As a result, the progress was cancelled, while the Choshu clan leaders were forced to flee to their home province.

In July 1864 a group of several hundred "irregulars" composed of *samurai* from Choshu supported by *ronin* went to Kyoto with the aim of asking the emperor to pardon the leaders who had been exiled after the so-called "kidnap plot." They camped outside Kyoto and awaited a reply from the emperor, but this was so long in coming that two further groups arrived; one as reinforcements, the other to try to keep things calm. At this delicate moment the Imperial court issued an edict announcing that the "irregulars" were to be punished, and started to assemble a military force to implement this, with troops assembling in the imperial palace's flower garden.

On August 20 1864 the *samurais'* patience ran out and the men of Choshu, by now numbering some 1,300, attacked the palace. The ensuing two-day engagement was the last great medieval battle in the world, with both sides wearing armour and armed with swords, bows, cannon and arquebus. As usually happened in such Japanese urban battles, fires soon broke out, consuming the highly inflammable houses and devastating several large areas of the city. However, the Choshu forces were completely defeated; while many escaped, some were captured, of whom 37 were beheaded.

The Tokugawa *shogunate* then decided to finish off the rebels once and for all, and a combined army headed southwards from Osaka. This was led by the *shogun* in person, and was organised and equipped on traditional lines. The people of the south, however, had been studying European fighting methods for some years and had obtained much foreign military equipment. Thus, when the *shogun* arrived with his army he found that the army of Choshu had thrown away its armour, swords and bows, and was not only armed with modern rifles and artillery, but it was also trained in European tactics. The *shogunate* forces were completely defeated and the young *shogun* died of exhaustion on September 19 1866. He was replaced by a new *shogun*, Keiki, who proved to be singularly ineffective and vacillating.

Meanwhile, the province of Satsuma had been initially somewhat less rebellious than Choshu, but events began to drive the two closer together and they concluded a secret military alliance in March 1866, greatly strengthening the anti-*shogunate* movement. Events now began to move rapidly and in the turmoil troops under the command of Saigo Takamori from Satsuma seized the emperor's palace. In the council that followed, the *shogun* was stripped of his

LEFT: The Russo-Japanese War (1904-05) was the first venture against a Western power, with Japanese forces showing a mastery of modern tactics, allied to the traditional bravery of the samurai. Here 1st Infantry Regiment covers itself in glory at the Battle of Nanshan (May 25 1904).

RIGHT: In this 1942 poster, the "samurai spirit" is invoked in celebration of the sinking of the British warships, Prince of Wales and Repulse on December 9 1941. Unusually, the flags of Japan's Axis partners, Germany and Italy, are also allowed to share in the Japanese Navy's glory.

remaining power, and the emperor was placed from the system of "dual government".

Fighting between the opponents and supporters of the *shogunate* continued with the 7-month long *Boshin* (Restoration War) culminating in the Battle of Veno (July 4 1868), in which the emperor's troops won and the power of the *shogunate* was broken forever. The emperor, Mutsuhito (122), regained the position of actual head of the government, took the name Meiji (= enlightened government) to designate his reign, and transferred the capital back to Edo, which he renamed Tokyo (= eastern capital). Meiji then compelled the lords of the great Choshu, Hizen, Satsuma, and Tosa clans to surrender their feudal fiefs to him (1869). Following a succession of such surrenders by other clans, an imperial decree in 1871 abolished all fiefdoms, which were replaced by centrally administered prefectures.

Farsighted statesmen such as Prince Iwakura Tomomi and Marquis Okubo Toshimichi managed to keep Japan clear of the European imperialism which was engulfing most other Asian countries at that time, and they set out to make Japan a world power. French officers were engaged to remodel the army; British naval officers reorganized and retrained the navy; and Dutch engineers supervised new civil construction in the islands. Thousands of Japanese were sent abroad to analyze foreign governments and to select their best features for duplication in Japan. As a result, a new penal code was modelled on that of France, while the education system was based on that of the United States. Conscription was initiated in 1872, and, finally, in 1876, their day being well and truly over, the *samurai* class of professional warriors was abolished by imperial decree.

However, not even the Imperial Rescript was sufficient to obliterate the memories, traditions and ethos of the *samurai* overnight. Thus, the concept of the *samurai* as a noble and selfless paladin – indeed, as the personification of the Japanese warrior spirit – persisted, returning on several occasions to haunt Japan over the following 100 years, frequently distorted to suit the ends of various cliques. This led to such episodes as the attempted coup by a group of junior officers and troops in February 1936 and, above all, to the events during the Second World War when the *samurai* tradition was deliberately invoked by the government and military leadership in order to encourage hordes of junior officers to carry out suicidal attacks on the ever-advancing Allied forces. There can be no doubt that these young men were sincere in their belief that they were the heirs of a fine and rational national tradition. Nor has the *samurai* tradition been without its adherents in the post-war world, when these older values have seemed to offer a simpler, nobler and more individualistic alternative to what appears to many to be a modern, depersonalised, greed-ridden, Western-dominated culture.

THE EMPERORS

EMPERORS IN PREHISTORY PERIOD								
	NAME	BORN	ACCEDED	AGE	DESCENT	ABDICATED	DIED	REMARKS
1	Jimmu		660 BC			–	585 BC	First sovereign; ascended throne on February 11 660 BC
2	Suizei	632 BC	581 BC		Youngest son of Jimmu (1)	–	549 BC	Killed eldest brother, pushed second brother aside
3	Annei	577 BC	549 BC	28		–	511 BC	
4	Itoku	553 BC	510 BC	43		–	477 BC	
5	Kosho	506 BC	475 BC	31		–	393 BC	
6	Koan	427 BC	392 BC	35		–	291 BC	
7	Korei	342 BC	290 BC	52		–	215 BC	
8	Kogen	273 BC	214 BC	59		–	158 BC	
9	Kaika	193 BC	158 BC	35		–	98 BC	
10	Sujin	148 BC	98 BC	50		–	30 BC	
11	Suinin	69 BC	29 AD	40	Third son of Sujin	–	70 AD	
12	Keiko	13 AD	71 AD	64	Third son of Suinin	–	130 AD	According to legend had 72 sons, 8 daughters

	Name	Born	Acceded	Age	Descent	Abdicated	Died	Remarks
13	Seimu	84 AD	131		A son of Keiko	–	190	Only son died young
14	Chuai	149	192		Nephew of Seimu	–	200	Died in battle, succeeded by widow Jingu, but she is not included on "official" list
15	Ojin	200	270		Son of Chuai's widow, Jingu	–	310	
16	Nintoku	257	313			–	399	
17	Richu	319	400			–	405	
18	Hanzei	351	406		Brother of Richu	–	410	
19	Ingyo	376	412		A younger son of Henzei	–	453	
20	Anko	401	453			–	456	Murdered his father (true heir) to gain throne. Murdered after 2 years on throne
21	Yuryaku	418	456		Brother of Anko	–	479	Bloodiest of all emperors
22	Seinei	444	479		Son of Yuryaku	–	484	
23	Kenzo	450	485		Younger of Richu's two grandsons	–	487	The 2 grandsons were found living as shepherds. Kenzo took throne with great reluctance
24	Ninken	449	488		Elder of Richu's grandsons	–	498	Reluctantly took the throne on his younger brother's early death
25	Buretsu	489	498		Grandson of Yuryaku	–	506	As wicked as Yuryaku. Died childless. End of line which started with Nintoku
26	Keitai	450	507	57	Descendant of Ojin (15)	531	531	Abdicated shortly before death; first emperor to do so
27	Ankan	466	531	65	Son of Keitai (26)	–	536	Died childless
28	Senka	467	536	69	Younger brother of Ankan (27)	–	539	Appointed Soga Iname as first minister starting parallel bureaucracy
29	Kimmei	509	539	30	Another son of Keitai (26)	–	571	
30	Bidatsu	538	572	34	Second son of Kimmai (29)	–	585	Died of sickness
31	Yomei	540	585	45	Son of Kimmei (29); half-brother to Bidatsu (30)	–	587	First emperor formally to become a Buddhist
32	Sushun	521	587	66	Nephew of first minister Soga no Umako	–	592	Assassinated on the orders of his uncle; buried same day
33	Empress Suiko	554	593	39	Widow of Bidatsu (30) and sister of Yomei (31)	–	628	First Empress Regnant. The power behind the throne was her nephew, Shotoku Taishi
34 35	Jomei Empress Kogyoku	593 594	629 642	36 48	Grandson of Bidatsu (30) Widow of Jomei (34)	– 645	641 –	Installed by Soga no Emishi The male heir was rejected and Kogyuku installed by Soga no Emishi in his place. On death of the Sogas, she abdicated but returned later as Saimei (37)
36	Kotoku	596	645	49	Brother of Kogyoku (35)	–	654	Kokyoku abdicated in favour of her brother, Karu, who reigned as Kotoku
37	Empress Saimei	n.k.	665	n.k.	Formerly Empress Kogyoku (35)	–	661	Restored by her son, Naka, she died on campaign
38	Tenji	626	668	42	Son of Kogyoku (35)/ Saimei (37)	–	671	Naka succeeded his mother as Tenji. One of the most powerful emperors. Appointed his friend Kamatari, as head of a new clan: the Fujiwara
39	Kobun	648	671	23	Son of Tenji (39)	–	672	Ruled for few months; defeated in battle; committed suicide
40	Temmu	622	673	51	Brother of Tenji (39)	–	686	Took 9 brides from influential families to ensure survival
41	Empress Jito	645	690	45	Chief of 9 widows of Tenji (39)	697	702	Abdicated in favour of her grandson
42	Mommu	683	697	14	Grandson of Tenji (39)	–	707	First minor to become emperor; died at 25
43	Empress Gemmei	661	707	46	Mother of Mommu (42), half-sister to Jito (41)	715	721	Mommu's son was considered too young and was passed over
44	Empress Gensho	680	715	35	Daughter of Gemmei (43), grand-daughter of Temmu (40)	724	748	Abdicated in favour of her nephew
45	Shomu	701	724	23	Son of Mommu (42)	749	756	Had been deemed too young to succeed in 707. After abdicating became a monk

HISTORICAL EMPERORS AND EMPRESSES REGNANT

	Name	Born	Acceded	Age	Descent	Abdicated	Died	Remarks
46	Empress Koken	718	749	31	Unmarried daughter of Shomu (45)	758	n.k.	Became mistress of head of Fujiwara clan.. After abdicating became a nun, but then took another lver, Dokyu
47	Junnin	733	758	25	Grandson of Temmu (40)	764	765	After an attempted coup against Koken's new lover, Junnin was forced to abdicate and exiled. He was assassinated in 765
48	Empress Shotoku	–	764	–	Formerly Empress Koken (46)	–	770	Having returned, Shotoku's lover, Dokyu, plotted to take power, but Shotoku died
49	Konin	709	770	61	Grandson of Tenji (38)	781	781	Died shortly after abdicating
50	Kammu	737	781	44	Son of Konin (49)	–	806	A great emperor, who moved capital to Kyoto, appointed first *shogun*, fathered 36 children
51	Heizei	774	806	32	Eldest son of Kammu (50)	809	824	Abdicated to become monk
52	Saga	786	809	23	Brother of Heizei (51)	823	842	Had some 50 children, but only first 7 retained royal status
53	Junna	786	823	37	Brother of Heizei (51)	833	840	
54	Nimmyo	810	833	23	Son of Saga (52)	–	850	Appointed his cousin crown prince, but was forced to change to his own son
55	Montoku	827	850	23	Eldest son of Nimmyo (54)	–	858	Became a puppet of his uncle. He had 27 children
56	Seiwa	850	858	9	Son of Montoku (55)	876	880	Maternal grandfather, Fujiwara Yoshifusa, became regent. Having abdicated he became a monk
57	Yozei	868	876	10	Son of Seiwa (56)	884	959	So violent that he was deposed aged 18, but lived until aged 82
58	Koko	830	884	55	Third son of Nimmyo (54); great uncle of Yozei (57)	–	887	Reigned 4 years, succeeded by seventh son, who was readmitted to Imperial status the day before his father's death
59	Uda	867	887	20	Seventh son of Koko (58)	897	931	Uda appointed a Sugawara counsellor, annoying the Fujiwara. After abdicating became an abbot
60	Daigo	885	897	12	Son of Uda (59)	–	930	Retained Sugawara as counsellor, infuriating the Fujiwara, who finally had him exiled
61	Suzaku	923	930	8		946	952	Acceded aged 8 with Fujiwara Tadahira as regent. No son, so appointed brother crown prince
62	Murakami	926	946	20	Brother of Suzaku (62)	–	967	Succeeded brother, but proved weak and saw rise of military clans in provinces
63	Reizei	950	967	17	Eldest son of Murakami (62)	969	1011	Had poor health, abdicated after just 2 years, but lived to age 61
64	En'yu	959	969	10	A younger son of Murakami (62)	984	991	
65	Kazan	968	984	17	3rd son of Reizei (63)	986	1008	Tricked into abdicating after just 2 years. Became a monk
66	Ichijo	980	986	7	Son of En'yu (64)	–	1011	Had a Fujiwara regent
67	Sanjo	976	1011	37	Son of Reizei (63)	2026	1017	Offended Michinaga, encouraged to abdicate
68	Go-Ichijo	1008	1016	9		1036	1036	Weak, dominated by the Fujiwara
69	Go-Zusaku	1009	1036	28	Brother of Go-Ichijo (68)	1045	1045	Another weak emperor
70	Go-Reizei	1025	1045	20	Son of Go-Suzaku (69)	–	1068	
71	Go-Sanjo	1034	1068	34	Brother of Go-Reizei (70)	1072	1073	Dismissed his Fujiwara counsellor and ruled firmly
72	Shira-kawa	1053	1072	20	Son of Go-Sanjo (71)	1086	1129	Ruled firmly but had very expensive tastes. Initiated system known as cloistered government
73	Horikawa	1079	1086	7	Son of Shirikawa (12)	–	1107	Emperor in name only, power lying with his father
74	Toba	1103	1107	5	Son of Horikawa (73)	1123	1156	Reigned from age 5 to 20
75	Sutoku	1119	1123	5	Son of Toba (74)	1141	1164	Died in exile, penniless
76	Konoe	1139	1141	5	Son of Toba (74)	–	1155	Sickly, died aged 17
77	Go-Shirikaw	1127	1155	27	4th son of Toba (74)	1158	1192	Acceded at 27 after severe fighting following Toba's death. Became a Buddhist priest in 1169
78	Nijo	1143	1158	16	Son of Go-Shirakawa (77)	–	1165	Was forced to flee from a coup d'etat dressed as a maid

	NAME	BORN	ACCEDED	AGE	DESCENT	ABDICATED	DIED	REMARKS
79	Rokujo	1164	1165	2	Son of Nijo (78)	1168	1176	Was first sidelined and then deposed in 1168
80	Takakura	1161	1168	8	Uncle of Rokujo (79)	1180	1181	Appointed crown prince when 6, Takakura was made the puppet emperor at age 8. Abdicated at age 20, died following year
81	Antoku	1178	1180	2		1183	1185	Drowned in the Battle of Dan-no-ura
82	Go-Toba	1180	1183	3	Brother of Antoku (81)	1198	1239	Go-Tuba was installed before his brother Antoku's death. Go-Tuba had little power, but played politics for many years after abdicating. Was finally exiled to Oki Island, where he died
83	Tsuchi-Mikado	1195	1198	4	Eldest son of Go-Toba (82)	1210	1231	Compelled to abdicate by his father and lived quietly until his death
84	Juntoku	1197	1210	12	Favourite son of Go-Tuba (82)	1221	1242	Joined his father in challenging the shogunate; ended his life in exile on Sado
85	Chukyo	1218	1221	3	Son of Juntoku (84)	1221	1234	Reigned for 70 days, before "abdicating". Died aged 17
86	Go-Horikawa	1212	1221	10	Son of Go-Toba's (82) elder brother	1232	1234	Died aged 23
87	Shijo	1231	1232	4?	Youngest son of Go-Horikawa (86)	–	1242	Died as a result of accident at age 14
88	Go-Saga	1220	1242	23	Son of Tsuchi-Mikado (83)	1246	1272	
89	Go-Fukakusa	1243	1246	3	Son of Go-Saga (88)	1259	1304	Allowed a limited spell on throne by his father, then obliged to abdicate. Became a monk
90	Kameyama	1249	1259	11	Favourite son of Go-Saga (88)	1274	1305	Became priest in 1289
91	Go-Uda	1267	1274	7	Son of Kameyama (90)	1287	1324	Became priest
92	Fushimi	1265	1287	22	Son of Go-Fukakusa (89)	1298	1317	
93	Go-Fushimi	1288	1298	11	Son of Fushimi (92)	1301	1336	Obliged to abdicate after 3 years. Became priest
94	Go-Nijo	1285	1301	17	Member of Daikaku-ji branch of Imperial family	–	1308	Died while still emperor, aged 23
95	Hanazono	1297	1308	11	Son of Fushimui (92)	1318	1348	Jimyo-in family branch. Obliged to abdicate in 1318, became priest in 1335
96	Go-Daigo	1288	1318	30	Son of Go-Uda (91)	–	1339	Sought to overthrow power of shogunate. Was forced to flee to Yoshino where he died
97	Go-Murakami	1328	1339	12	Son of Go-Daigo (96)	–	1368	Ruled atYoshino until death at age 40
98	Chokei	1343	1368	25	Go-Kameyama's elder brother	1383	1394	Ruled at Yoshino
99	Go-Kameyama	1350	1383	33		1392	1424	Was responsible for ending schism; returned to Kyoto where, by agreement, he abdicated
100	Go-Komatsu	1377	1382	6		1412	1433	Acceded in northern court in 1382; became undisputed emperor, 1392
101	Shoko	1401	1412	11	Son of Go-Komatsu (100)	–	1428	Despite agreement to alternate between families, Shoko was from north. A violent man and poor emperor
102	Go-Hanazono	1419	1428	9	Son of Shoko (101)	1464	1470	Reigned for 36 years
103	Go-Tsuchi-mikado	1442	1464	22	Son of Go-Hanazono (102)	–	1500	Reign included the Onin wars, which devastated the country. Could not afford abdication ceremony and died, still emperor, in 1500
104	Go-Kashiwabara	1464	1500	36	Son of Go-Tsuchimikado (103)	–	1526	Long reign dominated by civil war
105	Go-Nara	1496	1526	30	Son of Go-Kashiwabara (104)	–	1557	So poor that he had to write for cash
106	Ogimachi	1517	1557	40	Son of Go-nara (105)	1586	1593	His son died in 1586, but Ogimachi abdicated several months later being succeeded by his grandson
107	Go-Yozei	1571	1586	15	Grandson of Ogimachi (106)	1611	1617	Appointed Tokugawa Ieyasu hereditary *shogun*, but eventually the latter forced Go-Yozei to abdicate in 1611
108	Go-Mizunoo	2596	1611	16	Son of Go-Yozei (107)	1629	1680	

					Emperors and Empresses in the Historic Period			
	Name	Born	Acceded	Age	Descent	Abdicated	Died	Remarks
109	Empress Meisho	1623	1629	7	Daughter of Go-Mizunoo (108)	1643	1696	Never married
110	Go-Komyo	1633	1643	10	Son of Go-Mizunoo (108); half-brother to Meisho (109)	–	1654	Died at age 21, probably of chickenpox. Had no son, but one daughter
111	Gosai	1637	1654	18	Son of Go-Mizunoo (108); half-brother to Meisho (109) and Go-Komyo (110)	1663	1685	Chosen to avoid another empress, but was blamed for a series of natural disasters and forced to abdicate in 1663
112	Reigen	1654	1663	10	Son of Go-Mizunoo (108)	1687	1732	
113	Higashiyama	1675	1687	12	Fourth son of Reigen (112)	1709	1709	Died 6 months after abdicating
114	Nakamikado	1701	1709	8	Son of Higashiyama (113)	1735	1737	
115	Sakuramachi	1720	1735	15	Son of Nakamikado (114)	1747	1750	
116	Momozono	1741	1747	6	Son of Sakuramachi (115)	1762	1762	Momozono had 2 sons; eldest was 4 when he died
117	Empress Go-Sakuramachi	1740	1762	23	Daughter of Sakuramachi (115)	1770	1813	Decided not to have infant emperor; Go-Sakuramachi was selected instead. Never married
118	Go-Momozono	1758	1770	12	Eldest son of Momozono (116)	–	1779	
119	Kokaku	1771	1779	10	Great-grandson of Higashiyama (113)	1817	1840	
120	Ninko	1800	1817	18	Son of Kokaku (119)	–	1846	
121	Komei	1831	1846	15	Son of Ninko	–	1867	Died of smallpox
122	Meiji	1852	1867	15	Son of Komei (120)	–	1912	

					The "Northern Emperors" (1331–1392)			
	Name	Born	Acceded	Age	Descent	Abdicated	Died	Remarks
North 1	Kogon	1313	1331	18	Son of Go-Fushimi (93)	1336	1354	
North 2	Komyo	1322	1336	14	Younger brother of Kogon N1)	1348	1380	
North 3	Suko	1334	1348	14	Nephew of Komyo (N2)	1351	1398	Captured by southern forces in 1351 and held prisoner until 1357
North 4	Go-Kogon	1338	1351	13	?	1371	1374	
North 5	Go-En'Yu	1359	1371	12	Son of Go-Kogon	1382	1393	
North 6	Go-Komatsu	1377	1382	6	Son of Go-Enyu (N5)	–	–	After 10 years as Northern Emperor, Go-Matsu became sole emperor in 1392

APPENDIX B: THE SHOGUNS				
PERIOD	FAMILY	SHOGUN	LIVED	REMARKS
1185–1199	Minamoto	Yoritomo	1147–1199	
1201–1203		Yoriiye	1182–1204	Assassinated
1203–1219		Sanetomo	1192–1219	Assassinated
1220–1243	Fujiwara	Yoritsune		
1244–1251		Yoritsugu		
1252–1265	Emperor's sons	Munetaka		
1266–1289		Koreyasu		
1289–1307		Hisakira		
1308–1333		Moriyochi		Murdered on father's orders
1335–1357	Ashikaga	Takauji	1305–1358	Appointed by Kogen
1358–1367		Yoshinori		
1368–1393		Yoshimitsu	1358–1408	Became shogun at age of 10
1394–1422		Yoshimochi		
1423–1425		Yoshikadzu		
1428_1441		Yoshinori	d. 1441	Assassinated
1441–1443		Yoshikatsu	1433–1443	Eldest son of Yoshinori
1449–1471		Yoshimasa		1. Younger brother of Yoshikatsu 2. Ruled during Onin War
1472–1489		Yoshihisa		
1490–1493		Yoshitane	1465–1522	Defeated in battle; fled
1494–1507		Yoshizumi		Acceded at age 16
1508–1520		Yosihitane		Returned (see last but one). Deposed again; died in exile
1521–1545		Yoshiharu	1510–1550	Forced to flee; died in exile
1546–1567		Yoshiteru	1535–1565	Forced to commit suicide
1565–1568		Yoshihide	1564–1568	Acceded at age 2. Forced to flee, died soon after
1568–1573		Yoshiaki	1535–1597	Tried to rid himself of Nobunaga. Deposed; became a monk
1603–1604	Tokugawa	Ieyasu	1542–1616	1st Tokugawa shogun. Died in bed
1605–1622		Hidetada		3rd son of Ieyasu
1623–1649		Iyemitsu		
1650–1680		Iyetsuna		
1681–1708		Tsunayoshi		
1709–1712		Iyenobu		
1713–1716		Iyetsugu		
1717–1744		Yoshimune		First of Kii line of Tokugawa family
1745–1762		Iyeshige		
1762–1786		Iyeharu		
1787–1837		Iyenori		
1838–1852		Iyeyoshi		
1853–1858		Iyesada		Natural death
1858–1866		Iyemochi	1846	Acceded aged 12; died of exhaustion
1866–1868		Yoshinobu		A dithering man who resigned, then rebelled then resigned again

GLOSSARY OF TERMS

ashigaru: foot soldiers

ashigaru-taisho: *samurai* placed in command of a contingent of *shogunate*

bakufu: Japanese military rule; rule of the *shogun* (qv)

bakyu-jutsu: art of mounted archery

batto-jutsu: sword-drawing art that includes cutting rolled straw targets

betto: groom to a mounted samurai

bo-jutsu: fighting with staves

boshin: Restoration War (1868)

budo: the "way" of combat. Name adopted in the 20th Century for martial arts in general, with an emphasis on their peaceful aspects

bakurai-bishi: explosive escape aid used by *ninja*

bushi: warrior. Name given to all the warriors who made up families with a warrior tradition

bushido: the "way" of the warrior. A code of honour and social behaviour, which succeeded the unwritten code of the"way" of the bow and the horse

cho: unit of length (1 cho = 120 yards/109 metres)

chokuto: straight sword used in Japan's early history

daimyo: a feudal lord, who maintained numbers of samurai (qv) in his service, all of whom had sworn an oath of personal allegiance to him, according to the rules of bushido (qv).

daisho: *samurai's* two swords (one long: *katana*; one short: *wakizashi*)

daito katana: long sword

dô: a form of cuirass (ie, protection for torso)

doshin: constable

ebira: quiver

fuchi: collar, used on sword as a retainer for the *tsukaito* (qv)

fukini: cylindrical streamer used as an alternative to a *fukiniki*

giri: *samurai's* duty

gosanké: collective term for the three family lines (Owari, Kii, and Mito) descended from Ieyasu's three youngest sons

gunpai: war fan

habaki: collar at upper end of sword blade

hakama: divided skirt-pants worn by *samurai*

Heian period: era when Japan's capital was located in Kyoto (782 - 1184)

Heiji-no-ran: Heiji Incident (1160)

ho-o: "cloistered emperor"

Hogen-no-ran: Hogen Incident (1155)

iai-jutsu: art of drawing the samurai sword

jitte: a short mace used by doshin (qv) during the Edo era (qv)

jun-shi: literally, "dying with the master" in which retainers committed *seppuku* (qv) on the death of their lord, in order to demonstrate that their loyalty to him by accompanying him into the next world

kabuto: helmet

kaishaku: the attendant at a seppuku, who watched his principal slice into his own belly and was then responsible for beheading him

Kamakura period: when the capital of Japan was in Kamakura (1185-1332); also known as the "golden age" of the Japanese sword

kampaku: regent

kashi: oak

kashira: pommel-cap on sword

katana: long sword

katanakaji: swordsmith

katanatogi: sword sharpener

keikô: one of the types of armour worn during the Kofun era, using laces to secure scales (see also *tankô*)

ken-jutsu: the warrior's art of using the sword immediately it was drawn from the scabbard. Developed into the art of *kendo* (qv)

ken: an ancient, two-edge sword made before the 9th Century

kendo: the "way" of the sword, developed from the earliest times by *bushi* (qv)

ken-jutsu: art of the sword, particularly of using it as soon as it is drawn from the scabbard; transformed into the art of *kendo*

kikkosha: literally "tortoise wagon", a shelter used in seige warfare, accommodating up to a dozen men

komaku: protective shield for an individual archer

konida bugyo: commander of the supply train

koto: swords made before the Edo period

kubo-sama: name used by common people to refer to the *shogun* (qv) (also used by foreigners)

kunai: universal weapon/tool used by ninja

kusari-gama: small cresent-shaped weapon on a chain used by *ninja*

kuambaku: a title meaning "regent of the emperor" conferred on Hideyoshi in 1586

kyu-jutsu: the art of archery

kyuba-no-michi: the "way" of the horse and bow

makibishi: multi-pointed escape aid used by *ninja*

maku: screen partially surrounding the position of the commanding general on a battlefield, usually decorated with his mon (qv)

manriki-gusari: variant of *kusari-gama* (qv) used by *ninja* (also known as *fundo-gusari*)

mei: name of a sword

mekugi: retaining peg, securing hilt and tang of sword together

mochi-yari: spear

Momoyana period: 1573 - 1599, when *samurai* (qv) began wearing *daisho* (qv). Also the beginning of the *Shinto* (new sword) *period*

mon: family crest worn on *montsuki* (qv) and displayed in various ways on the battlefield

montsuki: kimono top worn by Japanese on formal occasions

muramasa: a sword-maker of the Muromachi period (qv), when production of swords was particularly intense

Muromachi period: 1392 - 1572, a time of constant civil wars

musha-shugyo: warrior pilgrimage

nabori: general's banner, laced to an L-shaped pole

naginata: a long pole ending in a curved blade, used by foot soldiers against horsemen, or against horses (by cutting their tendons, or disembowelling them). Also used by the wives of *samurai* and of warrior monks

naginata-jutsu: the "way" of the *naginata*

naidaijin: inner great minister (government title)

Nambokucho period: 1333 - 1391, a time when two emperors were vying for power in Japan

ninja-to: *ninja* sword

no-dachi: long sword

noroshi: signalling beacon

ninja: a group of specially trained men and women, usually from the lower classes, who were employed by the *daimyo* (qv) to assassinate enemies and infiltrate enemy strongholds

o uma jirushi: great standard, symbolising the location of the commanding general

ri: measure of distance (1 ri = approximately 2.4 statute miles/3.9 kilometres)

ronin: literally "wave people", a term applied during the Tokugawa period to master-less *samurai*

ryu: particular school or style of martial arts

saké: rice wine

sakoku: literally "closed country", the policy under which Japanese were forbidden to travel abroad and foreigners were prevented from entering Japan

samurai: a class of *bushi* (qv). The original *samurai* existed to protect their lord and were especially trained in martial arts, but the term was later applied to all *bushi* of a certain rank belonging to warrior families

sashini: small banner carried by individual *samurai*

saya: scabbard for sword

seki: guarded gate

sensei: teacher

seppa: oval washers on sword

seppuku: ritual suicide performed by the *samurai* in which they made deep cuts in their stomach before being beheaded. (Note: the expression *hara-kiri*, to cut the abdomen, more widely used in the West, is considered more vulgar.)

seto naikai: the Inland Sea

shiki = way station on a highroad

shikken: literally, regent. Title held by Hojo family members (1199-1333) who ruled on behalf of the *shogun*

Shinto: "new sword" — any sword made between 1596 and 1870

shin Shinto: "new sword" — any sword made after the Meiji Restoration (1870)

Shogun: literally "barbarian-subduing general" was the title given by the emperor to the *daimyo* (qv) who showed himself to be the richest and the most powerful of all the lords

shoto wakizashi: short sword (dagger)

shuriken: collective term covering various small projectiles used by *ninja*

so-jutsu: techniques of using the lance, and performed wearing the ancient armour of the *samurai*

sohei: warrior monks

tachi: generic name for a sword; many different types were developed over the centuries

taiko: title conferred on Hideyoshi after his death in 1598

tankō: one of the types of armour worn during the Kofun period, with cuirass, which was either rivetted or laced. See also *keikō*

tekemitsu: an imitation sword made of bamboo, carried by impoverished *ronin* (qv)

tsuba: sword guard

tsuka: sword hilt

tsukaito: thread used on sword hilt

tsuru: bow-string

tsurugi: sword with straight, double-edged blade

uchigatana: literally "inside sword"; the longer of two swords worn by *samurai*

wakizashi: short sword worn by samurai

yari: spear

yumi: bow

yumiya: bows and arrows

zanshin: samurai sensing danger

INDEX